Margaret Dunmore: or, a Socialist home. [A novel.]

Jane Hume Clapperton

Margaret Dunmore: or, a Socialist home. [A novel.]
Clapperton, Jane Hume
British Library, Historical Print Editions
British Library
1894].
205 p. ; 8°.
012629.ff.51.

The BiblioLife Network

GUIDE TO FOLD-OUTS, MAPS and OVERSIZED IMAGES

MARGARET DUNMORE

OR,

A SOCIALIST HOME

BY

J. H. CLAPPERTON

AUTHOR OF "SCIENTIFIC MELIORISM."

" Surely the wiser time shall come
When this fine overplus of might,
No longer sullen, slow, and dumb,
Shall leap to music and to light.
In that new childhood of the earth
Life of itself shall dance and play ;
Fresh blood in Time's shrunk veins make mirth,
And labour meet delight half way."
JAMES RUSSELL LOWELL.

SECOND EDITION

LONDON:

SWAN SONNENSCHEIN & CO.

PATERNOSTER SQUARE.

Crown 8vo, 443 pages, price 8s. 6d.

SCIENTIFIC MELIORISM,

AND THE

EVOLUTION OF HAPPINESS,

BY

JANE HUME CLAPPERTON.

"In the author we recognise an advanced thinker of a rare and high order."— *Westminster Review.*

"We earnestly advise all . . to read this admirable book."— *Weekly Dispatch.*

———

KEGAN PAUL, TRENCH & CO., LONDON.

CHAPTER I.

THE SCHOOL FRIENDS.

Leeds, May 5th, 1890.

My dearest Vera,

I obey an impulse to write to you on this my twenty-seventh birthday. Yes, dear, I am twenty-seven to-day; and I will tell you a secret, Vera—not the echo of a whisper of an offer of marriage has ever come my way! I smile when I look back to the period of my teens and remember my dear mother's useless caution, spoken in Scotch— you remember her Scotch, Vera?—it brings tears to my eyes when I hear it now: " Let a' the lads alane, an' your own gude- man will come to ye." No gudeman ever came to me; so I must belong, doubtless, to that surplus million of women for whom dame Nature, affluent as she is, has nevertheless provided no husbands. The absence of courtship disappointed me, however; romance was what I looked for in my girlish life, and I confess I was often very, very miserable until the lucky day, about two years ago, when the railway accident near Settle made an era in my life, by giving me my precious friend, Miss José.

B

I

I have never told you much about her, Vera, because you must see and know her for yourself, and because you could not understand what she has become to me, without my giving you a history of my thoughts and feelings—and that is a difficult thing to do. When we passed a long night together in that snowed-up train, I was in the "sturm und drang" period of existence, and plunged—to use George Sand's phrase—in egoistic sorrow. I was weary of culture, for what to do with it I could not clearly see; frivolous pleasures had palled upon me; romance was nowhere, except on the pages of novels, which I despised myself for reading; religion had ceased to comfort, being mixed with a theology my intellect questioned and doubted at every point; and as for life itself, with all its refreshing breezes of altruistic interest in human welfare— individual, social, political, universal,—it, alas! was utterly over-shadowed by my own insignificant little personality, and I suspect my mood was one of—Perish all mankind, since I, Margaret Dunmore, am unhappy.

> "There's nothing in the world can make me joy:
>   Life is as tedious as a twice-told tale,
>   Vexing the dull ear of a drowsy man."

How Miss José plucked out the secret of my discontent I cannot tell. She asked me no questions, so far as I remember, but, next day when we parted, with mutual wish and resolve to meet again, I am convinced that my innermost being was like an open book before her mind's eye, although not one incident of my outward history had she learned from my lips. Well, dear, since then we have had frequent and intimate inter-course, and whether I attribute it to that alone, or not, I now declare to you I am no longer Margaret the unhappy, but, a Margaret whose youth has been restored to her, and who is panting with enthusiasm to greet her early friends and bid them good cheer.

Why have you and I been silent so long, my Vera?

"Is all the counsel that we two have shared—
The sisters' vows, the hours that we have spent—
Is all forgot?"

Not so : our natures are faithful and **true** to the core, and the motion, whatever it is, that has drifted us apart, is a surface current only, under which there flows the stream of our deep affection, calm and undisturbed.

Last night I was at a concert in our Town Hall, and, strange to say, there sat next me our old school companion, Jessie Blair. She it was who told me Vera is about to be married, and I suffered a pang half remorseful, half jealous— Has Margaret in her preoccupation neglected her Vera? or has Vera forgotten Margaret?

Write to me, dear, and show me your heart, as I wish with all my heart to show **you** mine.

Your faithful friend,
Margaret Dunmore.

———

Liverpool, May 6th, 1890.

Dear old Margaret,

Twenty-seven is old, is it not? But I don't mean that, only that old times came back to me when I read your darling letter, and I would have liked to fling myself into your arms and have a good cry.

Jessie Blair's tale is not true; but it is true, and an awful secret, that I am engaged. She meant Mr. Scott, a horrid old bachelor who bores me with his talk whenever I meet him, and has taken me to the theatre once or twice. I was awfully silly to let him, but Joe cannot bear me to mope. He says he ought never to have told me how he loves me, since it is impossible for us to marry for ever so long; and that I must not stay at home and be miserable on his account, but go about like other girls, and keep dear mother cheerful. Perhaps he will see he is wrong when he hears this gossip about Mr. Scott. I knew the Abercrombies and others were saying that he paid me attention, but I did not know they had us engaged yet! Oh, dear! what a worry it all is, and how disgusting that a girl can't walk or talk with a man but someone is sure to say she is going to marry him; and worse still, a girl dares not speak out when she really loves a man, and let him and all the world know it. Secrets are the most hateful things in life; but, indeed, life is hateful altogether; and I do wish we were back in our childish years, when you were the clever girl at school, and I her stupid little friend whom she called Sunbeam, because, though not clever, I was at least happy and bright.

There is no sunshine in me now, dear, and sometimes I feel wicked. I am angry with God when I think of dear mother's sufferings, and what happened to her five years ago is what people, you know, call a Providence. But what was the use of a Providence that let a cab-driver get intoxicated and throw down an innocent lady in the streets, and hurt her so much that she is an invalid for life, and suffers pain every day?

Then, why couldn't Joe have had money instead of Mr. Scott? He doesn't want it much; I am sure no girl can be waiting to marry him; and he gives me dreadful frights. Dear mother likes him to come in and sit talking with her in the evenings, but if he were to propose, all that would come to an end, I suppose, and he would be angry and disagreeable, and perhaps mother would find out about Joe. I feel it wrong that mother does not know about Joe, now; but he says it would be cruel to tell her, since he has only £100 a year, and his little Vera is a lady with white hands unused to labour. I'm not proud of my white hands myself. I've often stood and watched a workman's wife scouring her doorsteps, or washing her husband's shirts, and thought if I could only do all that, I might be Joe's wife at any time. And after all, what can I do that is better? I play a little, but you know

my music is very poor, and not worth the money and time it
has cost to teach me ; and I speak French and German—what
is the use of that, when I never go abroad, and foreigners here
all speak English ? I can look like a lady of fashion, but that
means that my dress is pulled back in front, and bunched out
behind, that my sleeves and gloves are too tight, and my heels
are too high.

Even Joe laughs with me at some of our silly fashions, but
he was vexed one day when I wanted to wear cotton gloves.
And if I were to insist on being cook or parlourmaid, and
appear before him in a get-up suitable for the work, goodness
gracious ! how Joe would frown.

What a bother ; here is Mary, to say Mr. Scott has called and
mother wishes me down.

Good-bye, dear Margaret.

Your loving

Vera.

P.S.—I was twenty-four last week, and Joe gave me a little
gold cross to wear, because, he says, he is my cross.—Dear
fellow, I love him so.

Leeds, May 8th, 1890.

It seemed old days indeed, to get such a nice long letter
from my Sunbeam, like herself, very practical, but careless !
You forget, my dear, that I do not even know your Joe's surname, nor of what nature is his occupation. That he is good
and lovable I am quite sure, since my clear-eyed Vera
loves him ; and I am prepared to take him to my heart as a
brother. Tell him, at once, that I know your secret, and that
Margaret Dunmore will never rest till you and he are husband
and wife, a happy and humdrum (that means contented)
married pair.

Yours tenderly,

Margaret.

SCENE.

A plainly furnished parlour in a small house at New Terrace, Liverpool.

A young man stands in a depressed attitude, leaning an elbow on the mantel-piece. He is tall, fair, blue-eyed, with a noble forehead, thin lips, and a gloomy expression.

A rapid foot and rustling skirts on the staircase are heard ; the young man's attitude changes—he is a model of manly eagerness and strength.

Vera Ward enters, an open letter in her hand, and the light of love in her eyes.

"Joe, dear," she cries, and offers a kiss.

In responding, Joe Ferrier's countenance alters ; a beam of almost womanly tenderness plays upon the thin lips.

"Look here, Joe, you know all about Margaret Dunmore, and how dearly I love her ; see, she has written me these letters, and you will easily understand from the first one, why I told her all about our engagement ; but look, this note came only this morning, and Margaret says—'I will never rest till you and he are husband and wife.' What can she mean ? She *must* see some way to help us, Joe, else she would never say that." And pleading eyes are raised to the young man, who, with one arm round her waist, is bending over her shoulder to read the words to which she points.

A variety of expressions sweep across his face—pleasure, doubt, inquiry, annoyance, irritation, pride. He moves his arm, turns round, and placing his large, sensitive hands on her two shoulders, looks into her eyes and says sternly,—

"Margaret Dunmore is rich: it would ill become me, Vera, to take money from any one, remember that. I must either make a living for my wife myself, or leave her with her mother. How is your mother this morning, my love ? You have not yet told me that ——"

For the remainder of the day the Sunbeam droops.

Little Vera bears a fresh thorn in the delicate flesh of her most sensitive part—her affections. Yet, of the why and the wherefore of that wound she says nothing, and scarcely knows anything.

CHAPTER II.

FRANK AND ROSE.

From Dick Oswald, to Frank Ray,

On board the Celestial, bound for China,

May 6th, 1890.

WE'VE had confounded bad luck in weather, Frank; but for that, I meant to drop you a stave by the "Koh-i-noor," which passed us ten days ago, for, I declare, old fellow, I never saw you so down in the mouth as when we parted in Liverpool Docks.

You asked my advice—well, it's briefly this: Marry that girl right away, and emigrate. She is no high-flier, who won't soil her fingers to do a stroke of honest work: and, by Jove, the old country is too crowded by half. I don't say, Try China, where the human swarms like bees! But be a farmer in the States, man—that's the life for you; and a deal healthier one, let me tell you, than stewing at figures, these eternal pounds, shillings, and pence, in a beastly den of an office. It may suit your new friend, Joe Ferrier, with his smooth chin and well-trimmed nails; but Ferrier is not Frank Ray.

Your father, you say? Well, there's no denying he will feel cut up a bit at first: but look at my mother, now; you know what she wanted—to keep me tied to her apron-strings, in that blessed old Kenilworth, all my life! Only think of it, Frank, what a life for me! When she found it could not be, she gave in like a trump; and now you go and see her at

8

Southport, when I am not present, to blush at the praises of her sailor boy! Judge for yourself if she be not content. Her crib, too, is ship-shape, and it pleases her, the dear old soul, to show off the kickshaws I pick up for her here and there.

Believe me, we can't give in altogether to the old ones; so pluck up spirit, and carve out a destiny for yourself—that's my advice.

If you go to the States, let me know.

Yours heartily,

Dick Oswald.

———

Frank's father would indeed have been cut up, had Frank followed the advice of this friend of his school-boy days. Mr. Ray had been brought up in the school of Robert Owen, in whose mills his parents were workers. These, with many others, drifted outwards when the happy settlement at New Lanark was broken up, and Sandy Ray went to sea. At forty he married, and soon after lost his wife in giving birth to their only child. Sandy settled in Liverpool and lived wholly in and for his child. He has always been a sober, cautious, thrifty man, strong in his somewhat narrow affections, and shrewd in his intelligence. He managed to get into a good situation in a shipping office, and saved money as well as gave his son an education that surpassed his own, further than his had surpassed that of the boy's grandparents.

Frank is now, externally, a broad-shouldered, fair-haired, fine-looking man, and internally, a fellow of culture and taste. He is broadly social too; not merely in feeling but in intelligence, for, added to the strong mental qualities, there has ever been in him an absence of the reticence which springs from personal vanity or pride, and he revels in that play of intellect—the give and take—that society promotes, and only free natures enjoy.

One troublesome element of character mars at intervals his peace of mind, and that is an instinctive impulse and desire to rove.

He knows this to be inherited from his father, and fostered by tales of adventure poured into his boyish ears by that father whose one thought had been how to please and gratify the lad.

The sensational, originally strong, was a chord well played upon, before Frank was ten years old, and the tones to which it vibrated were all the more delightful that the old sailor ceased to distinguish clearly between the true and the false. All that brought a smile to his darling's lips seemed true to him. Frank, I have said, has culture, but he is no great Greek or Latin scholar. His father's set idea, persistently harped upon was—" My son is to be a scholar ; " but at fourteen the boy took his father to task on the subject—" What is a scholar ? If you mean I'm to keep at Greek and Latin all my life, I will not, Dad, indeed I will not. It is all rot, learning to make Latin verses ; and although I do want to know about these old Greeks and Romans—what they did, and how they lived— I don't care to speak their old language and waste time on learning horrid declensions. I will be a gentleman, if you like, and a well educated one too, but not an old fogie like Dr. Grumpus, who is always reading ; and I know they call him a scholar."

Mr. Ray removed his son from the classical to the science course in school, and Frank took to the new training like a duck to the water. Physics, mechanics, geology, chemistry, botany, zoology, physiology—all these presented fields in which that eager young intellect ranged, assimilating mental pabulum, and building up a structure of knowledge fitted to its own individual capacity. Long after leaving school, the young man pursued his studies by means of evening classes, and at twenty-six the result was culture in no ordinary degree, although Frank would still say, " I am no scholar."

This vigorous intellectual life promoted physical health; pure air and exercise were self-chosen. The lad traversed the neighbourhood in search of natural products, and dedicated all the spare time at his disposal to that healthful and innocent chase.

His absorption, however, presented one danger: the intellect might dominate the heart until the latter should lose vitality, and be unable to throw out delicate tendrils to entwine and cling about his fellows; and undoubtedly the human being is warped whose nature does not tend to make of life a garden of holy affections, as well as a rich soil and sure footing for the tree of knowledge. Frank had never been in love.

But one Sunday in January, 1890, he entered a new phase of life, and the particulars of this transition I am bound to relate.

Theological contentions have always been distasteful to Mr. Ray, and whether he holds many or few dogmas, I fancy no man knows and no man would venture to ask.

When religion is spoken of, he indicates disapproval and pious veneration by solemn silence, or at most, by a significant shake of the head. He assumes a devout Sabbatarian aspect when he dons his black clothes, and walks, with measured step, to the Presbyterian chapel, his son accompanying him as a matter of course.

Frank had learned to be present there in body, whilst

absent in mind. The latter portion of him did not wander upon mountains of vanity, but roved over a wide area at the sea level, peering into many hidden corners of nature's secrets.

He had a habit of holding over any problem that specially puzzled him, to be tackled and perhaps solved on these Sunday mornings; for, strange to say, he was conscious of superior acuteness when in that quiet place, his beloved father at his side, humanity under restraint all around him, and solemnity prevailing.

On the Sunday referred to, however, Frank was present, in every sense of the word, his acuteness directed to a phenomenon before his eyes.

At right angles to his father's pew there was one containing a lady of mature age and rather stern aspect, three children—one of them being lame,—and a girl above twenty, on whose eyelashes trembled two teardrops made brilliant by a sudden gleam of sunshine.

These crystal drops are wonderfully significant little finger-posts on Frank's path, altering the course of his destiny; but of that he knew nothing.

Intellectual curiosity is what they have aroused. Why should a girl cry in church? Every phenomenon has its antecedent cause, but where was the cause of these tears?

The face was turned to the pulpit, and devout attention was its expression. Frank eagerly listened to the preacher's words, then scanned the text: "He said unto his father, My head, my head. And he said to a lad, Carry him to his mother.

"And when he had taken him, and brought him to his mother, he sat on her knees till noon, and then died."

Can the sickly-looking child at her side be foredoomed;

and do the teardrops betoken anticipation of his early death ?

Frank looks keenly at one after another of the pew-occupants, and in a few moments he has discovered that kinship is not the bond of union between Rose Karrattray and Mrs. Benson. Rose is an alien in the family, in some dependent position ; probably (and his guess is a correct one) the lady-help or nursery-governess.

Now it belongs to Frank's healthy physical and mental development to make stiff resolves—not hastily, but deliberately, and carry them out perseveringly. He did so now. He resolved that he would get to know the girl, and ascertain from herself why those tears were shed, and if he found some permanent cause of suffering, that he would try to help her.

Three months later he had compassed that end. He had learned from Rose's own lips that the crowded Rectory down in Devonshire, which was her home, was that morning receiving back into its bosom, beaten and battered but not slain, the hero of the family, its pride and joy, her elder brother Basil. He had been a brilliant student, had taken his degree as doctor, and sailed for India. But the action of the climate from the first was deleterious to his highly strung nerves, and a slight sun-stroke was the final catastrophe that left him no resource but to return to the shelter of his childhood and "sponge," as he termed it, upon his already burdened parents, a broken, disappointed man.

How Rose and Frank passed through many stages of acquaintanceship into close intimacy in the three months I need not minutely describe.

The gentlemanly youth found ways and means to ap-droach the girl without impropriety or offence to her dignity. Mrs. Benson respected the church eldership and social position of Mr. Ray, and made no objection to his son's visits to her house, and occasional walks with Rose and the children, when, with his strong arm propelling the invalid's carriage, extended circuits became possible to the pedestrians, increasing the pleasure of all. Frank was a charming companion to the children, for, whatever attracted their wayward fancy—from the ships to the sea-urchins in their rambles along the shore—from the bird on the wing to the caterpillar or the tiny cup-moss, when the explorations were inland,—he had something to tell of each, which was fairy-like in its fascination, although, of the nature of instructive fact.

Mrs. Benson saw clearly the bent of the young man's mind, and she was a practical woman, not averse to benefits where her children were the recipients.

It so happened that at times the invalid boy was asleep and the little ones at play; then Frank and Rose were virtually alone, and their intimacy advanced by strides.

In temperament Rose resembled Frank, whilst her culture and training had been wholly different. No wonder she presented to him a new study of transcendent interest.

Within the Rectory of Westbrook a babe was born at intervals of never more, sometimes less, than eighteen months; the normal state of the gentle mother was one of feeble health, and Rose had been her prop and stay from very tender years. Self-repression was the daily attitude of the little maid, whilst she made herself generally useful all round. From her father she inherited a logical cast of mind; from her mother artistic qualities of no mean order.

Her delight in pictures, poetry, and music was instinctive ; and, since to make an independent career outside the home was a necessity imposed on her by the numbers within, the Rector would have done well to train and launch Rose as a musician. But economy was an imperative consideration, and the Rector was a man who applied all his logic to the squaring and fitting of practice to old dogmas under new conditions, rather than to the examination of new doctrines in the light of simple truth. Hence the equality, in justice, of his children's claims upon his purse escaped notice ; to be a nursery-governess must suffice for Rose, whilst he strains every nerve to find ways and means of giving his son Basil the expensive college education which ended disastrously, as we have seen.

Rose, however, was educated. Her development took place in a school of experience infinitely preferable to the hard, mechanical, routine-loving day-school or boarding-school of the ordinary British maiden.

There were no divided interests in *her* child-life ; all the objects of her love were close within reach, and the perpetual promptings to think of and for others and subordinate her own wishes to theirs, increased her power of loving day by day. When I say self-repression was her inward attitude, I may be misunderstood ; it was so to the onlooker only. Rose would have told us she never made sacrifices at home. But in the many little choices that even a child must make day by day, Rose's choice was independent of the ego ; her sweet nature made her wish to do what others would like best ; and thus, when first brought into contact with Frank, she was emotionally of a high type of womanhood ; the best fruit of an advanced civilisation.

Her desultory lessons, given sometimes by a governess,

sometimes by her father, were highly prized, and she was permitted to guide the line of study according to her own bent.

The æsthetic was what she craved in all directions—to see the beautiful with her inward eye, rather than to collect facts or acquire knowledge.

The Rector had travelled in his young days, and could describe to her the treasures of art that Greece and Italy contained. She became familiar with the history of art. The renaissance was the fairy-lore of her imagination, and when the dark-haired curly head bent over the pages of Vasari in the Rector's library, a child's heart beat sympathetically with the griefs and triumphs of these ancients—the heroes of art,—whilst the memory stored up knowledge of their achievements.

Of the physical sciences Rose knew nothing at all, and for Botany she had, at one time, the prejudiced dislike that often accompanies ignorance. Basil had hurt her æsthetic instincts when he plucked the flowers to pieces to ascertain their structure, bruising brutally, as she thought, the delicate petals and destroying their beauty for ever.

Frank taught her differently. His science was full of the reverence that is born of love for the special study; and as he dissected before her eyes a blossom or an insect, the noble spirit of inquiry, the veneration for truth that dominated the act was a mental atmosphere that Rose could appreciate. Her prejudices were subdued, and she learned to perceive that the sense of beauty should be supported by knowledge of nature's marvellous modes of action, and not deal only with the superficial—the lovely forms and colours that adorn the surface.

To Frank the most thrilling pleasures of his life had come when instructing Rose. Her docile disposition and newly awakened interest in science made her mind like a sensitive plate to every impression, and the varying emotions of his soul were reflected from her violet eyes, to double or treble the force of their original charm.

His vanity too was gratified, or rather, I should say, his feeling of male supremacy—that consciousness and love of power which, in barbarous ages was a masculine attribute of supreme importance to the feebler sex, while now it is only obstructive to true union, even when, as in Frank's case, it exists as a rudimentary instinct, nothing more. Frequently, however, the position was wholly altered. If discussion fell upon life, and the conduct of life, Rose was teacher, and Frank the humble disciple. Great was his surprise when he discovered that, young as she was, her mind had dwelt upon many grave problems of human life with earnestness and philosophic insight: subjects which he was accustomed to turn from indifferently or with an airy lightness!

Her genius for loving made very real to her everything that touched the happiness of mankind; and although, in her home her sphere of action was very limited, her sphere of thought was by no means so.

The pressing questions of the day—the poverty of the masses; the vice and misery existing in large towns; the pressure of competition in industry; the adulteration of industrial products; the necessity for emigration;—were talked of in the Rectory, and Rose's tender heart made her grasp the fact of the vital importance of these questions, and place them at once in the sanctity of her gravest thoughts and most religious desires and feelings.

The power of music too, over Rose, was an enigma to Frank. He knew perfectly that the strains of Beethoven

c

soaringly carried her into regions whither he could not follow.

On one occasion Mrs. Benson had permitted him to take Rose to a concert of sacred music. To have charge of a girl without chaperone was a novel experience, and Frank was elated. Never had he felt so strongly and delightfully that they belonged to each other: but behold, the moment the music began, Rose seemed to alter; a sense of distance oppressed him, he was restless, dissatis-fied, tried vainly to attract the attention of the absorbed girl, finally plucked her sleeve, when she turned upon him a face of surprise, without recognition! 'Twas but an instant, but to him a space of time leaving an indelible impression, ere the absent soul fluttered back to the windows and smiled out at him through the gentle eyes

Frank had never again asked her to go to a concert.

It was, perhaps, well for Rose that her duties in Mrs. Benson's house were of a commonplace order, leaving comparatively little time for meditation, and that one of these duties was to engage in healthful frolicsome play with the little ones, whom she dearly loved; for a girl who at seventeen is capable of being saddened by a father's remarks on increase of crime amongst the masses, and would weep in sympathy with the griefs of suffering humanity at large till she sobbed herself to sleep, is in danger of falling a victim to hysteria, or some other morbid action of the nervous system.

The practical, however, pressed hard upon Rose, and even in her abstract moments, guided her to a principle of supreme importance, viz., this: that society will be reformed only by reform of the individual, and that each individual in his or her own little corner, may do something towards that divine end, by possessing a noble ideal of life, and shaping conduct to that ideal.

Consequently Rose's mind had been greatly exercised on ideals of right conduct in different circumstances; and she had a curious way of referring to her father and mother in a voice resonant with religious veneration, as though their having brought her into the world was a claim on her life-long service and gratitude.

This was to Frank a strange point of view.

Amongst his many masculine acquaintances he had never chosen for his friends any of the triflers and empty-headed mashers with whom all our cities in the present day abound; but the spirit of the age in youth—and it affects more or less all ordinary minds, even those of good type—is one of bumptiousness or personal independence, and Frank's friends were wont to enlarge on filial claims and rights, and to be silent on filial duties. Hence, Rose's point of view was a novelty to Frank's intellect, and it affected his moral fibre in a subtile manner of which he was himself unconscious.

But my reader will now understand how it came to pass that, although, when standing on board the "Celestial," with Dick Oswald, an intense longing to range over the world and see life under new aspects had swept over him, and the oppression of his monotonous office work had momentarily stifled him, so that every molecule of his flesh as well as the half-choking voice cried out to Dick, "How shall I break my fetters here and be free, like you, to roam abroad?" Yet when Dick's letter reached him, he flushed with indignation, and flung it summarily into the fire.

Ten minutes later, Frank was by his father's side, saying, in a tone of unusual tenderness, "I think you look a bit seedy, dear Dad; let's run down to Southport, and have a ramble on the sands together."

CHAPTER III.

MR. SCOTT.

FROM Miss José to Mons. Henri Martin, her friend of many years.

(A free translation.)

Leeds, June 9th, 1890.

My dear Comrade,

It were indeed vanity to compare Thérèse José with George Sand, yet precisely as she remonstrated with and scolded her beloved friend, Gustave Flaubert, so, I approach and am ready to reproach you!

Her words are pointedly appropriate: "To wish for near death or for a long life is weakness . . . Say inwardly: 'The Flaubert of to-day must be superior to that of yesterday, and that of the next day must be stronger and more lucid still.' . . . You will gradually enter upon the happiest and most favourable age of life—old age. . . . . My point of view is, in fact, to perceive the incessant gravitation of all tangible and intangible things towards the necessity for what is good, noble, and true. I do not say that mankind is on the road to the loftiest regions of good, yet I believe it, in spite of all."

And again, "You will not succeed in stamping out human folly. . . . As for myself, I look upon it with motherly

20

eyes; for it is that of childhood, and childhood should always be sacred."

Patience, my good friend! Be patient with yourself and the world at large. The clear-eyed George Sand, with her noble ideal of what society should be, and her cataclysmal experience—revolution after revolution, the retrograde Empire, the Commune, the dillydallying Republic—was, at seventy, serene and hopeful still; and shall we, whose epoch displays much more creditable features, gnash the teeth in despair?

True, men are foolish, many of them brutal, as you say; but, do you not perceive, to destroy is no longer the supreme instinct, but to organise, to recreate?

Can we, who are old, guide them a little in this momentous matter? There is the question to put to ourselves. We are both Socialists, though you deny me that portentous title: but see, my friend, let us not quarrel about names.

You maintain that in 1789 the world was nearer to Socialism than it is now. I reply: Not so, for the effort then, and many efforts since then to give birth to Socialism, were abortions, nothing more. Now, the advent of that child of the ages is taking place on all sides every day, only it is a puny weakling; and you, wise as you are in some things, had the folly to expect it would spring like Pallas Athena from the head of Zeus, armed cap-à-pie.

Our Socialism, believe me, is the legitimate child of freedom, although as yet a mere babe in swaddling clothes. The world is too old now to worship at an infant's shrine. Our attitude is no longer supplicatory, but tenderly protective. Humanity will cherish, nourish, patiently uphold the baby footsteps of its future king; in one word, it perceives that childhood is sacred.

But I must drop these figures of speech. Ah! my friend, you are not of the shopkeeper British nature, so practical, so intense—to make money! You are my confrèrr. You understand what is an idea, and enthusiasm for an idea; so I do not say, pardon my figures. I have told you, from time to time, of my charming young friend Margaret Dunmore. She is no British shopkeeper; her mind is not of the counter—you understand? And in these last days she has become a Socialist. Of your sort? Nay, I do not say that. She would not help you to pull down society and build hastily on its ruins a social structure that, however sublime in conception and extensive in execution, would in a few years totter helplessly, and fall to the ground! Hers is the Socialism of the new era, which she carries as a babe in her bosom, and does not expect it to accomplish any great things. She allows it must creep and walk before it can run.

You know perfectly, my friend, the questions on which we differ and have contended for years.

You adopt the banner of Revolutionary International Socialism.

I object to your term Revolutionary, because to my mind it suggests violence, and I, as a Socialist, abhor violence, and think it wholly unjustifiable.

I object to your term International, because, until there is virile strength in many individual groups, or socialistic centres, international relations are premature, they will only serve to dissipate energy.

You "seek a change in the basis of society, a change which would destroy the distinctions of class and nationalities." I seek a change in individuals—in human character, and primarily (in order to bring about the above change) an alteration in home-life. I hold that for true progress the first and most necessary step is the creation of a modern domestic system, favourable to the bringing into the world humanity of a new type. This humanity will spontaneously reject competition in industry, and rise above class distinctions. It will organise itself into the true society of the future, viz., a peaceable Socialism that has never trodden down or destroyed a single

relation of life, never exercised violence or imbrued its hands
in blood.

"We shall not live to see that Socialism," you say? Ah!
there, my Henri, we are agreed. Like Moses, you and I may
stand on the top of Pisgah, and, with our mind's eye, view the
promised land; but for us, as for Moses, the fiat goes forth—
"Thou shalt not go over thither!"

All the more, my friend, let us set our faces towards the
promised land, and by our own individual efforts, lay down
some of the solid framework of that bridge by which the next
generation will pass over to possess it.

You, Henri, would dwell for ever upon Pisgah. What I
supplicate is, that you come down from those lofty regions of
ideal delights, and help us in the modest and menial labour of
building the bridge!

Now comes the delicate point of this somewhat verbose
epistle; the key-note that will test the harmonies of our life-
long friendship. Will you, Henri Martin, sacrifice your
domestic independence, and, for one year, on trial, become
member of a Provincial Communistic Group—ladies and gentlemen who intend to live, rather than preach, Socialism; and
who hope to rear children of a purely Socialistic type?

You are well acquainted with the various experiments
already made by mankind in this direction, and their all but
invariable failure. Nevertheless philosophers recognise the
march of events which may make possible to-day, and easy
to-morrow, what was impossible ten, five, or even one
year ago.

Sceptical of our success you may be, but give in your ad-
herence, Henri, to this new endeavour, and come, visit me here
without delay to show yourself not a theorist—a dreamer only,
but a practical socialist, willing and able to cope with the
dry details of a homely but important economic experiment.

Come to us, my friend! Come!

Your THÉRÈSE JOSÉ.

From Mons. Martin to Mlle. José.
                    National Liberal Club,
                              Victoria Street, London,
                                        June 11th, 1890.

Ma bonne Amie,
              We are not in the stone age, nor in the iron
age, but we are in the age of—la femme !

I fear me, Thérèse, your friend Henri Martin is too old a
fish to swim contentedly in that limpid pool of which you tell
me : but you and that charming Mademoiselle Marguerite
fling over one the delicate silken meshes of your feminine
attractions, and what can I do but obey your commands ? I,
a Frenchman ! I shall be with you upon Friday after midday.
                    Yours, till then,
                              HENRI MARTIN.

                    ————

"You do me injustice, Vera, indeed, you do me
injustice," exclaimed Joe Ferrier, placing his large hand
over the little one that lay upon his arm ; " of course I
want to marry you as soon as possible, but think, dear,
only think of it—a home in which you and I would not be
alone together ! What kind of home would that be ? Is
our private life to be a public one ? Are we to eat in
public, spend our evenings in public, and have no domestic privacy ? I know Miss Dunmore is a sensible girl, I
don't deny that ; but women, as a rule, are such idealists,
and you confessed yourself she wrote poetry at school, and
nonsense of that sort. You are carried away by her
notions, Vera, and she is not practical."

"Good heavens ! do you know she means to have no
servants in the house ? ' The ladies,' she said to me, ' will
undertake the domestic labour, upon a mutual service
basis !' " and placing Vera upon a garden seat, he wheeled

round in front of her and asked in strident tones of moral indignation, " Am I going to let you cook, and iron, and black my boots ? "

In a low voice, but very eagerly, Vera cried, " No, no, Joe, Margaret never said I was to black your boots ; she told me that in America gentlemen black their own boots ; and indeed I would let you do that, if only you will let me cook and iron, and wash dishes. You can't think how nice it is to do these useful things,—far nicer than doing fancy work, and reading novels, and making calls. Oh ! I hate making calls, and mother sent me to-day, Joe, to call on Mrs. Jardine. Mother says she's a superior woman, but I'm sure I don't see how she is superior, unless it is that she has two footmen—one to open the door, and another to show you upstairs ! I felt quite sorry for the men, it seemed such idle work. I am sure Margaret will never ask us to do any idle work of that kind in her 'Unitary Home.' She said there would be no callers, for we should not have time for it. How delicious, Joe, to have no time ! I have always too much time, and when I am expecting you, the time is dreadfully long and tiresome."

Joe's face softened, he sat down beside Vera, then suddenly started to his feet again. Some people who, like themselves, had been sauntering in the suburban garden, began running towards the highway, and when Joe turned in that direction he saw a crowd there which seemed rapidly increasing.

He spoke hastily to Vera, in a tender but somewhat peremptory tone : " Stay where you are, dear, till I return ; I'll find out what is wrong ; " and quickly left he side to vanish in the crowd.

A feeling of painful loneliness and suspense seized upon

Vera, but in a few moments Joe was again before her, saying, with authority, " You must get home, Vera, at once. Take the upper way—the crowd might jostle you; and I have to go with the fellow who's hurt."

" Oh! Joe!" cried Vera, almost in tears, " is anybody hurt? Who is hurt? Will he die?"

" No, no, dear, don't take on like that; a fellow, Spiers, I met him in the Free Library: he's come to grief somehow; I don't know whether he was on the tricycle or the horse, but there has been a smash, and a doctor there has sent for an ambulance car to take him to the infirmary. He thinks there may be concussion of the brain. I must go with them, for no one knows Spiers but myself."

Whilst saying this, Joe was hurrying Vera along the upper garden path, where he left her again with a hasty " Good-bye, dear; I will not be able to see you before to-morrow, if then."

In dismal spirits, Vera pursued her way home, and as she entered the room in which her mother sat half-recumbent in an invalid-chair, she was ill prepared to exercise patience under the frequent fault-finding, which, although directed towards her daughter, was, in the poor lady, simply an outcome of her inward state of discomfort and pain.

"Where have you been, Vera?" Mrs. Ward said fretfully; " and why did you stay out so long? You really must make up your mind to part with Lucy. If I were mistress in my own house——"

" Oh! don't say that, mother," exclaimed Vera; "you are mistress, you know you are."

" No I don't, and Vera, what a habit you have of interrupting me: what was I going to say? Oh! if I were mistress, Lucy would have been dismissed long ago.

How often have I told you how slow she is in answering the bell when you are out. I do not like my visitors kept standing on the door-steps; and Mr. Scott must have thought he was never to get in. By the bye, Vera, he can take you to the concert to-morrow evening."

"I am not going to any concert to-morrow evening, mother," interrupted Vera, and she looked at her mother with a dogged expression that altered the whole character of her face.

Mrs. Ward moved restlessly, raised herself on her elbow, and said, "Vera!" in a rasping tone that fell like an abrasion on her hearer's delicate nerves, "your rudeness to Mr. Scott is what I will not permit. He is to call again to-night, after tea, to show you the programme and tell you what places he has taken; and I insist upon it, Vera, that you treat him politely, and behave as a lady ought to behave to her father's friend."

Vera's answer was flung at her mother in a high-pitched key, as she hastily unbuttoned and took off her gloves— "Ladies hate to have favours thrust upon them; *real* gentlemen ought to know better than take a girl about, and pay for her as if she were a barmaid. I will not go to concerts if I can't pay for them myself. It is cruel to ask me, mother." And a wave of self-pity broke the last words into a sob. Mrs. Ward fell back on her pillows, and with an air of abandonment of all responsibility in the actions of a contumacious child, said harshly, "I don't pretend to understand you, Vera: in my young days a girl was proud and happy to be admired and cared for by a good man, whether she meant to marry him or not; but since that entanglement of yours with Joe Ferrier ——"

A sudden sweep of skirts checked the speaker, and before she could look up, a slam of the door and a flying step on the staircase told her that Vera had fled and left her mistress of the field.

The poor lady collapsed upon her pillows, and tears of utter helplessness welled feebly from her eyes, until she dropped asleep, and breathed softly in a blessed oblivion.

Meanwhile Vera, alone in her chamber, was kneeling by the bedside, sobbing passionately. That word entanglement might, at this period of her life, have been called the bête noire of Vera's existence.

During the three weeks of a visit that Margaret Dunmore had paid to Mrs. Ward, the latter was gently and cautiously enlightened upon the subject of Joe's and Vera's engagement; and the secrecy that had tried Vera in many ways was finally dispelled. But the invalid had long accustomed herself to suck a few drops of comfort into her chequered life from the belief that, sooner or later, the worthy man whom she leant upon as her counsellor and friend would win Vera's consent to take them both to his beautiful home, and be rewarded in time by the grateful devotion of his child-wife. That she must no longer indulge in this dream was to Mrs. Ward a new element in her diffused sense of general discomfort; and since the whole phenomena, subjective and objective, of Vera's future, was to her a mass of confusion in which Mr. Scott and Joe Ferrier were inextricably intermixed, she had stumbled into the habit of speaking of her daughter's engagement as an entanglement! little knowing that the word was touchingly expressive of the tangle presented by her own thoughts, feelings, and desires, and in no way applicable to Vera's relations with Joe.

Vera had no clue to her mother's state of mind, and the offensive expression seemed nothing less than an insult to her beloved Joe. She had become painfully sensitive and irritable in temper at every mention of his name, and the harmony between her and her mother was now constantly ruffled on the surface, although the deeper bond of tender love and devotion could never be destroyed. Nor was this all. The most immoral result of the strained position lay in her feeling towards Mr. Scott.

Exasperation is the term by which to describe it. The entanglement imputed to Joe was frankly laid by Vera on Mr. Scott's broad shoulders. *He* was to blame for each and every domestic conflict as it arose; and as Vera had very little critical faculty by nature, and her education had not developed the reasoning powers, she drifted unconsciously into the most irrational judgment of an innocent person and into personal animosity towards him.

The thought of him now gave some relief to her overcharged nerves of sensation. To be angry with her mother was intensely painful; to blame Mr. Scott was pleasurable by comparison. If *he* had not called, Lucy would have escaped censure as well as herself! An excess of burning indignation thrilled Vera throughout, and a shower of silent anathemas fell harmlessly on Mr. Scott's devoted head. Then followed a wave of gentle feeling towards her mother—compassion, anxiety. Had the excitement of the tiff between them made her ordinary suffering greater? Vera sprang to her feet, threw off her hat and mantle, bathed her eyes, and ran quickly downstairs.

Her mother's gentle breathing reassured her. She stole softly to her side, arranged the pillow beneath the sleeping head, kissed the forehead, murmuring, "Poor dear darling mother!" and sped upstairs again, to seat herself at a writing-table and pour out all her troubles to Margaret, in a letter which, to the writer at least, seemed satis-

factorily conclusive in its impeachment of Mr. Scott as a
monster of iniquity, specially created to cause quarrels and
all manner of other miseries to—" her unhappy, but loving,
Vera ! "

She was about to add a postscript, when her mother's
bell caused her to fling down the pen and quit the room.

Mrs. Ward was awake and suffering. Vera tended her
gently, and could now bear the fretful tones with perfect
equanimity.

By-and-by, when she was easier, Vera rang for tea; and
when that meal was over and the table cleared, she brought
some fancy work, and sitting by her mother's couch, strove
to amuse her with a simple relation of the events of the
day.

Mrs. Ward leaned back and half-closed her eyes. She
showed coldness towards her daughter, and listless indifference to all she was saying, until the accident was
mentioned; then she sat up and eagerly asked questions
that Vera was unable to answer.

The thought of another's sufferings awakened interest,
and the poor invalid's self-conscious and somewhat selfish
mood was at once exchanged for one of sympathetic
kindness.

She wished Joe would come to tell if Mr. Spiers were
better; she hoped the doctor in whose hands he was would
prove capable, and the nurses attentive. These young
lady-nurses one hears of nowadays, she had no confidence
in them. Girls were, as a rule, so giddy. The good old
ways were, in her opinion, the best, and so on. The dear
lady spoke as though nurses of the old-fashioned type
had never been girls at any period of their life !

In the midst of this talkative breeze, Mr. Scott's quiet
ring, and Lucy's opening of the outer door were not heard

and before Mrs. Ward and Vera were aware of it, that bald-headed gentleman was in the room, and closely observant of the emotions his presence excited.

Vera rose to her feet with an air at once startled and aggressive, suggestive of the absurd notion that Mr. Scott's short figure and benevolent countenance acted on her as a red rag to a bull!

"What have I done now to make Vera angry?" thought Mr. Scott; and his keen eye meeting Mrs. Ward's look of mingled pleasure, bewilderment, and timid anxiety. "Oh! oh! there has been some bickering about me," as quickly followed.

He shook hands with both, notwithstanding Vera's stand-off air, and then innocently drew from his pocket the concert tickets, little dreaming that they played any part in the scheme of these hidden emotions.

"Miss Vera," he said, "you wished to hear the new oratorio, and I have been so fortunate as to get ——."

"Oh! thank you, Mr. Scott!" the girl interrupted him, "I am not going to leave mother to-morrow evening; and besides, I don't ask gentlemen to take me to places. If I did say I wished to hear the oratorio, that was not meant."

"My dear Miss Vera, it is no trouble, only a pleasure to me to take you; surely you know that?" And as he spoke, a frank look of perplexed surprise made Vera hang her head and hastily take up her work. "If you prefer not to go," Mr. Scott continued, "of course I will not urge it, but your mother said she could spare you."

"My mind is made up"—Vera flung her words at him as though exasperated, "so pray say no more; I am sorry you took tickets, you should have asked *me* first."

"The tickets are of no consequence at all, Miss Vera;" and turning from the girl, whose flushed cheeks warned him to drop the subject, Mr. Scott addressed Mrs. Ward, and with delicate tact, drew her into conversation on topics of general interest.

Whilst thus engaged, Vera slipped from the room and went upstairs, where, after adding to Margaret's letter a postcript which was a mere childish outburst of anger against the inoffensive Mr. Scott, she closed the epistle and sent it to the post.

Then placing herself at the window, she tried to read, whilst her ears were sensitive to the distant hum of the voices below, and her eyes kept watch, lest Joe should suddenly round the corner of the Terrace, in spite of his farewell words to the contrary.

Meanwhile Mrs. Ward was having one of her good times.

Her husband had been a keen politician, and when his former friend told her the political news of the day, and discussed with her public questions, whose importance she fully appreciated, the past came vividly before her, and the sufferings she had subsequently experienced were momentarily blotted out. She talked well and earnestly for an hour, and when Mr. Scott said kindly, " You are tired now ; I will ring for Lucy, and you will get to bed," she made no objection, but bade him good-night with a serene and happy aspect.

Mr. Scott did not leave the house. When the invalid had retired, he mounted the staircase, rapped at the boudoir door, and entered without waiting for Vera's permission to do so. That she was still cross and angry with him was only too evident ; but there was in his manner, as he seated himself beside her, a masculine decision that subdued her into silence.

" How is your friend, Miss Dunmore ? " he began ; " I hope you and she are soon to be together again ? A friendship formed early and continued through life is a very precious thing, Miss Vera; your father and I had just such a friendship as yours with Miss Dunmore, begun at school, you know, and' broken only by death. You look surprised;" for Vera glanced up at him, and with a smile— "did you think schoolboys are little ruffians with plenty of fist but no heart? Your father was older than I. I looked up to him as you do to your friend, and leant upon him and loved him dearly. Ah! Miss Vera, to lose one's friend is a crushing blow! I trust you will suffer no such loss; but I want you for one moment to imagine that Miss Dunmore had married, and then died, leaving a husband and a child—tell me, how would you feel? Would not your Margaret's child be very precious to you? Would it not become part of your life to be kind to her? And if your little kindnesses were rejected?"

"Oh! Mr. Scott," cried Vera. She was looking at him now earnestly, and had forgotten her pettish little self. "I will go with you to the concert, please, and I *don't* mind what people say, or if you *do* pay money for me. I didn't think you loved me so much for father's sake."

"Stop, Vera, do not misunderstand me, pray: I wish you," said Mr. Scott, "to know our precise position to one another. When you were a babe and a prattling child at my knee, I loved you most for your father's sake. But that is a long time ago, now, and you were not always the distant, haughty little Vera that I have known in the last few months; you were cordial, frank, and free; I grew to love you for your own sake, and because I had seen you in the presence of young men for whom you did not care, and had never seen you with Mr. Ferrier, and knew nothing of your engagement to him, I made a mistake. I thought it possible you might one day

D

willingly marry a man old enough to be your father."
Vera had cast down her eyes ; two little tears stood in
them, and strange to say, she did not shrink from Mr. Scott
—respectful attention was what her attitude expressed.

"Now that I know you love Mr. Ferrier and he loves
you, what your father's friend desires, and will promote
if he can, is your happiness with him. At my age, Vera,
men are not passionately jealous! You may trust me, dear
child, and give me your friendship." With a sudden
impulse, the girl held out both her hands to him and
tried to speak, but only choked a little.

"There, there!" Mr. Scott said, shaking and dropping
the hands; "that is quite enough about an old fellow like
me. Now Vera, I want to hear of that communistic
scheme of Miss Dunmore's. She is a very sensible girl,
and if she can organise an associated home, there is no
doubt that comfortable and even luxurious living would
cost much less in that way than it does to individuals
whose homes are like mine or your mother's—dependent
upon servants, you know. Ferrier is a young man, and of
course has not saved money yet; but you and he might
marry without imprudence, if you joined Miss Dunmore's
group, and naturally your mother would go with you;
she has no objections, she tells me."

"Did she say that? Oh! Mr. Scott," cried Vera,
"how glad I am that you do not think it such a foolish
scheme. But Joe I'm afraid will never consent! He
says I am not to black his boots, and he thinks Margaret
will make me! but I am sure she will not."

Mr. Scott drew in his breath with a slightly hissing
sound, and stared abstractedly, as though seeking for
some invisible object and finding it in human shape too
tightly laced and strapped; then recovering himself:

" Well, well, Vera," he said, " Mr. Ferrier must have time
to look at it all round, and if he cares for my opinion, you
know, he will have it. But I must bid you good-night:
why, it is already almost ten o'clock !" He held out his
hand, but Vera did not quit him. She accompanied him
downstairs and to the outer door, and there, as she bade
him good-bye, an overwhelming sense of her injustice towards him, an impulse of mingled self-reproach, remorse,
and hero-worship demanding instant expression, brought
the colour to her cheeks, her eyes swimming in tears to his,
and culminated in—an offered kiss !

" God bless the child," said the lonely bachelor, as he
turned towards his desolate home. And the child:
had she learned to love him in half an hour? Scarcely
but, at least the mortal enemy had become to Vera her
dearest foe !

When her head touched the pillow an hour later, she
fell into the dreamless sleep, the profound repose of youth
and health. But her mother had only the broken rest
that was usual with her. In an access of suffering,
Vera went to her, and before leaving she said softly:

" I am going with Mr. Scott to the concert, mother;
he is not angry or disappointed now."

" Ah, Vera! Mr. Scott is a kind friend to us both,"
said Mrs. Ward; and Vera replied, " I know that, dear; I
am never going to quarrel with him any more."

In again dropping to sleep, her confused sensation was
one of generosity—she had forgiven someone, and had
had, somehow, a good deal to forgive !

CHAPTER IV.

HOW JOE CAME TO THINK DIFFERENTLY.

THE accident that befell Isaac Spiers did not differ from other events of human life in that it was fruitful of consequences; but, it differed from some, in this respect— that these consequences were in a large measure beneficial.

The concussion of brain was a slight one, yet, since Mr. Spiers was an extremely intelligent man, there was aid to science in the clear account he was able to give of the loss of memory which the accident caused. Strange to say, although he could remember every circumstance subsequent to the moment when consciousness returned, there was a definite period—about an hour and ten minutes—previous to the accident, of which his brain possessed no record: and it is by close observation of similar experiences, that human knowledge, regarding the mental processes and the deliberative formation of memory itself, is slowly being built up.

But other consequences were less general. They were personal to Joseph Ferrier, and direct in their bearing upon his subjective moods and objective actions throughout life.

During the three and a half weeks that Mr. Spiers was in the infirmary, there were few days in which Mr. Ferrier

36

did not visit him. The latter was working hard in a mercantile office, and had only a limited time each day at his disposal; nevertheless, ten minutes, if no more, could be spared for the cheering of a fallen and disconsolate comrade.

I know nothing of the fellow's history, was what Ferrier frequently thought; and certainly there had been no interchange of personal confidences; still, he was aware that Spiers was a creature of retiring habits, possessing few, if any, relatives or friends; and he was ready to sacrifice his own, and perhaps Vera's pleasure also, rather than let the sick man miss the comfort that his presence gave, especially during the tedium of convalescence.

Of Vera no word had been spoken. Although Joe had plenty, as we see, of manly charity, he was neither apt to give nor to seek the tender sympathies that bind together beings of more sensitive temperament; and he was not by nature frank, but reticent.

Imagine, then, his surprise, when upon one occasion, as he was leaving hurriedly to go to Vera, the patient interrupted his apology with, "My dear fellow, you have only been too good; the lady, whoever she is, to whom you are engaged, must wish me at Jericho:" and on Joe's exclamation, he added, "But don't let me detain you now; I will explain when you come again how I discovered that delicate relation—not by gossip, you may be sure."

On the following evening the explanation was given. "I followed you one day," Mr. Spiers said, "into the gallery of pictures. The girl who hung on your arm seemed very happy, and you, naturally, were engrossed with her and did not perceive me. For an hour at least, I observed you both closely, though avoiding your eye."

Here the sick man raised his head a little from the

pillow of the convalescent couch on which he was stretched, trying in a fumbling way, to place it so that he might better put into focus his companion's face. The latter took no notice of the movement, but looked at him with an intent, rather doubtful, expression.

"It was your masterful air towards the lady, Ferrier, that told me you were engaged to her, and gave me a clue to one reason, at least, why *I* have never had any success with the sex! It is a queer page of history the world is writing just now. Evolution goes fast, and very unequally. The majority of women, especially sweet and gentle ones like your friend, lag behind in the race. The subjection of women epoch is, inwardly, their historical position, and a man must be masterful to win their love! Of course in courtship, even matrimony, it is all right with natures such as yours and hers; but by and by the difficulties will appear."

"What do you mean? Do you suppose Miss Ward and I will quarrel when we get past forty?" said Joe, with a sparkle in his eye, indicative of wounded pride.

"My dear fellow, no! I suppose no such thing," said Spiers; "I was thinking of your future children and the absolute impossibility, I consider it, of rearing the young, suitably to the period in which their maturity will be passed, in these accursed English homes of ours, with their narrow, prejudiced mental atmosphere, their spurious despotism without, their real anarchy within! Truly! a survival of the—no longer fit. Do not you see, Ferrier, it is a shameful anachronism, in the present day, to live and go on rearing children according to the old regime! We are galloping towards the break-up of this archaic system, the outbirth of a new republicanism, socialism, communism—goodness knows what, but in any case an

-ism in which equality, not of capacity, but of sentiment, of reciprocal action will be a *sine qua non.* What policy is it, then, but a suicidal one, to create in individuals the old bond—protection and tyranny on the one side, subjection and obedience on the other? Why, man! the tendency in human nature to that bond is neither more nor less than a primitive organ of the social body, which, left rudimentary, will prove harmless, but developed, may impede, nay, ruin, the new system."

As Mr. Spiers uttered these words rather excitedly and with a flushed cheek, a lady-nurse entered the room. She was startled by this new phase in her usually silent patient, and gave Ferrier the hint to bid his friend good-night.

Joe, to tell the truth, was relieved by the dismissal. Mr. Spiers' last sentences had been a mere talking in the air, so far as he was concerned; but two facts had laid hold of his consciousness; he wanted to turn them over in his mind. First, Spiers had seen something to dis-approve in his manners to Vera! second, Spiers treated it as a matter of course that he, Ferrier, should take into consideration a non-existent family, and shape his present course in relation to that family! Hitherto Joe had felt it a matter of delicacy to treat that distant contingency from the negative standpoint, and ignore it.

His parting words to Mr. Spiers were these: "The education of my children—ah! that knotty point may stand over till we meet again. Sleep well, friend; don't let these unborn imps disturb your rest!"

It was with a smile that he left him, but, emerging from the infirmary, to move along sloppy streets amidst dripping umbrellas—for the evening was wet—his reflections fell naturally into a sombre groove. How is a man ever to marry at all, thought he, if children are to be taken into account as well as money, social position, and all the rest of it? Then, suddenly Margaret Dunmore and her Unitary Home rose into his mental vision; a thrill of distaste, if not disgust, passed through him, followed by a different impulse—curiosity. Had Spiers, in his travels, ever come across Icarians or Shakers, or any of these queer American Communists? I'll ask him, thought Joe. Another vision presented itself—Vera in communistic dress, *i.e.,* loose trousers and a rather scanty skirt falling just below the knee! A few days previously, Joe had dipped into Mr. Nordhoff's volume on "Communistic Societies of the United States," and had lingered with a non-appreciative aspect over the illustration at page 282.

His next thought was—I would be a brute to consent; when, instantly, memory supplied a fresh picture—Vera in ordinary attire; her garments fashionable, at every point—comme il faut; her sweet face animated, and words bubbling from her lips, "If only you will let me cook, and iron, and wash dishes,—it is so nice to do useful things—I hate making calls."—— At this moment a persistent newsboy carries his point; Joe stopped to buy his evening paper, and the train of his reflections was prematurely broken.

Two evenings later he was again in the infirmary with Mr. Spiers, who, in the interval, had made great progress. After some preliminary talk, Joe led up to the subject in his mind: "I say, Spiers," said he, "what go-a-head people the Americans are! They are Republican enough, surely, to suit you? As for their home life—the domestic hearth and that sort of thing, which you don't like,—why, they live mostly in hotels, don't they, or stupid communes, or something? Have you seen any Shakers or Perfectionists, or the Devil knows what, who seem to pig together and make fools of themselves, with their Communal nonsense?" The last words were spoken severely. Virtue affronted lurked in the tone.

The complex marriage of the Bible Perfectionists of Oneida Creek had shocked and disgusted Joe, who, with the usual injustice of superficial thinkers, calmly overlooked vital distinctions, and classed together the various groups of American Communists as though all were alike in theory and practice.

Mr. Spiers detected and instantly showed up this fallacy. "From where does your information on communal life come, Ferrier?" he asked. "To accuse Shakers of leading unseemly lives is too absurd. Their homes are pictures of wholesomeness and propriety—scrupulously neat and clean; and as for conduct, Shakers are perfect models of orderly behaviour; they are celibates too, as of course, you know. Amongst the Oneida and Wallingford Perfectionists, celibacy is not the habit of life and the marital custom is retrograde, certainly; and not, as they suppose, a step of advance into civilised freedom. Still, it is not brutish instincts, but a childish Theology that has led them astray: and after all, though their form of marriage is a lapse backwards, there is no lapse downwards for the children! That I can say with confidence. In all Communities that I have visited, wherever there are children, these are well cared for—fed, clothed, trained, educated, disciplined; brought, at nineteen or twenty, up to the level of the mental and moral attainments of the group. Now think for a moment, my dear fellow, of the mass of corrupt and corrupting child-life at the base of our social structure, and our miserable School-Board attempts to deal with it! What has the Foster Education

Act done for us?   Killed off perhaps, by strain on weak
nerves, a handful of our surplus numbers, and sharpened
wits for the odious, senseless fray—the fighting, scrambling,
grabbing, gambling of what we call the industrialism of
civilisation! Bah!"   As he spoke the last sentences with
growing acerbity, Mr. Spiers' voice had become sharp and
penetrating.   His nurse heard; and bringing to him a
draught of some kind, she adminstered, with it, a very
necessary caution; then glanced with a strangly suspicious
eye at the innocent Ferrier.

Miss Freeman was what Mons. Henri Martin would have
called Dévote.   From the first the uncomplaining gentle-
ness of the sick man had won her heart.   As a study, he
was a puzzle to her, because his patience under affliction
had no piety for its origin, so far as she could see : her
offers to read the Bible to him were politely declined.
As a case, he was not only interesting, but creditable ;
his recovery thoroughly satisfactory ; and doctors are apt
to be lavish in praise of a nurse's skill, when the nurse
is young and pretty.   Miss Freeman had come to acquire
a sense of property in her patient that was extremely
pleasurable ; but behold, Joe's visits had brought in a
disturbing element, the cause of which was not apparent :
a word of significant import struck upon her ear; that
word was " Commune," and its associations were positively
alarming—petroleum! dynamite!   No wonder Miss
Freeman looked at Joe with suspicion, and as she passed
from the room, pondered how she was to protect her good
little simple patient from the designs of this wicked
conspirator !

It was Mr. Spiers who renewed the communistic talk ;
Joe would have gladly avoided it.   He saw Miss Freeman's
glance, and felt sensitive to Spiers' criticism, although he

was quite too gentlemanly and kind-hearted to resent a word spoken by a sick man. Moreover, that horrid proposal of Margaret Dunmore's—that he should marry Vera and live in a Commune! What if Spiers discovered it, and took part with the women against him?

"I'll keep that dark," said Joe, to himself. But behold! in ten minutes' time a new emotion impelled him to make the disclosure:

"If we must be contemptuous," Spiers had said, "at least let us scoff like honest Englishmen at faults and failings nearer home, leaving America alone. It is a young country, and demands at our hands the consideration of age for youth. It is for age to solve the weighty problems of our times, such problems as how to produce and properly distribute enough food for all; how to create decency, comfort, refinement, culture, in and throughout a nation's entire structure from top to bottom. Now, what is our hoary-headed Britain doing to that intent? Little or nothing at all, but talk.

"To be sure, it occasionally forks out from well-lined breeches-pockets some £70,000, to build a People's Palace, and brags of it as one of the biggest things the civilised world has yet seen!

"Big, forsooth; what is bigness? Nothing to boast of, that I can see. That patronage by the rich of the poor is the biggest sham of man's invention. It is not that way, believe me, that social reformation will arise. Commend me to small beginnings full of vitality, self-sacrifice, personal responsibility. Shakers, with their quaint simplicity, their insect-like industry, are nearer the true path—childish though they seem—than all our philanthropists, however princely the fortunes they bestow. The valleys of England, Ferrier, are filled with dry-bones, when the earth is crying out for flesh and blood and vigorous life. If only one could see experimental action— communal homes, or anything else, in which lies an energizing, germinating principle, then would I believe in the shaking of the dry-bones, the speedy outbreak of a vernal spring. ‚‘Come from the four winds, O breath, and breathe upon these slain, that they may live.’”

The eyes fixed on Joe had become dreamy, yet, so sadly earnest, so yearning, that to resist was impossible.

“Would that cheer you?” cried Ferrier. “Well, you won’t have long to wait, then. There’s a Commune of some kind going to be started at Peterloo, I believe. They want me to join; but, upon my soul, I thought it was all women’s nonsense. I had no idea you would take the thing seriously. Well, by Jove, if you joined I might try it too, for a time.”

Genuine pleasure sparkled in Mr. Spiers’ face, as he questioned Joe, who, to tell the truth, knew very little of the details of the scheme; and presently, in response to the latter’s feeling, rather than words, he said:

“I do not wonder, Ferrier, that your instincts revolt. Nature shaped you for the upper levels of an Oligarchy, not exactly for the dead level of Communism. Still, you are young, the temperament phlegmatic, adaptation might conquer, if the motives sufficed. Have you independent means? Can you marry at once, in any case?”

“Oh, no,” said Joe; the colour coming to his cheek. “We must wait a year or two.”

“And Miss Ward,” queried Spiers; “is she willing?”

“Well, yes; she thinks she might like it. The fact is, she doesn’t like waiting.”

Joe felt as a traitor, in answering thus. He had an

instinct, though he could not have put it into words, that the simple, pure-minded Vera was a little disgraced by her readiness to become wife before masculine urgency required it of her.

But Mr. Spiers was evidently unconscious of this fine susceptibility, or, at least, took no notice of it.

"I think, then, Ferrier," he said gravely, "that your course is clear. Miss Ward is, probably, more modern in type than you are. With so strong a motive for effort, I don't see but what you may rub off the ugly corners of character that impede adaptation, and may hurt your happiness a little at first. You must not expect a bed of roses! If Communes are not that, neither is life anywhere, in this age of rampant struggle and discontent. Humanity has got to be moulded, you know, to be prepared for a better and happier stage of the world's history. Let *us* begin with ourselves. Goodness knows I am willing to try any new experiment, if only your ladies will accept me as eligible when they know about me—what little there is to be known."

For three-quarters of an hour longer the conversation continued, Mr. Spiers speaking much the most—the little silent man had suddenly become talkative. He told Joe many particulars of his private history; he criticised and animadverted on Joe's own personal pride, and other idiosyncrasies in so kindly a spirit that, to take offence was impossible; although, clearly, he had been taking stock from the first of his young friend, making observations and drawing his inferences, which were by no means pleasing to Joe's amour-propre.

When the last words had been spoken, Ferrier turned homewards. He felt slightly humiliated, but, to Margaret Dunmore and her communistic scheme more compliant than he had ever dreamed that he could become.

CHAPTER V.

EXCELSIOR.

On approaching Primrose Bank Terrace, Leeds,—a row of eleven small houses without any beauty, unless their exact resemblance to one another be considered such,—a stranger will look in vain for primroses; but, he will certainly perceive here and there, all along the line, "Apartments to Let," in legible, and, in some cases also, ornamental writing.

The monotonous plainness, yet the neatness and trimness, the white blinds, the netted-work curtains—at a few points the æsthetic touches in window decoration, these give a significant aspect to the Terrace. It speaks as pointedly to the stranger of genteel poverty, of a humanity, especially in the form of widowhood, struggling bravely, under burden of small economies, to uphold the cheerful dignity of life; as the many magnificent mansions of the suburbs speak to him of capitalism, and the questionable æsthetics achieved in and by humanity of the capitalist type.

At No. 9, Primrose Bank Terrace, there was no appeal for lodgers in the window.

The widow there had for five years enjoyed freedom from anxiety concerning a lodger, for Miss José was in full possession of the first floor, and her weekly payments,

46

though small, were regular. They sufficed, when added to the pension Mrs. Plimsoll received—her husband had been a Captain in the army—to cover the expenses of herself, her juvenile handmaiden, and her two sturdy, somewhat voracious boys.

Miss José was seated on a low chair, her feet on a footstool, in the first-floor parlour of No. 9, about five o'clock one afternoon of June, 1890.

She was engaged in earnest, animated talk with her friend Henri Martin, when a visitor's rap, followed by a murmur of voices in the tiny hall, announced an arrival, and Margaret Dunmore entered the room with a glad exclamation :

"So you are at home, dear ! I was so anxious to see you that I slipped away from the afternoon tea, at Mima Rose's; but I feared that naughty man—" and she threw a saucy glance at Mons. Martin, "might have spirited you away to some frivolous amusement, or some horrid revolutionary meeting or other, before I could get here."

She had crossed the room with an elastic step, and, kneeling on the footstool, kissed her friend warmly on both cheeks; while Mons. Martin, who returned the saucy glance with interest, stood looking at the two with a very appreciative air.

He liked a pretty picture, and such was before him at the moment: youth and age, both beautiful in themselves, encountering with all the delicate flashes of light and colour which affection, sympathy, and joy send forth.

Margaret was beautifully dressed, in rich material of olive tint, and after a fashion of her own.

"You dress like a frump," had been said to her only the day before : and if comparison with her girl critic is to supply our data for the definition of frump, one must be tilted forward from the ankles, bulge out stiffly behind, and be cramped above the waist, in order to avoid that disparaging similitude!

Margaret's movements were easy and graceful. Her skirt fell in elegant folds around her person; and, as she sprang to her feet, and removed her hat, she embodied Mons. Martin's ideal—he was a good judge of the female form—of noble, refined womanhood, emancipated from the bondage of senseless, often hideous, fashion.

"See," she said brightly, holding out two volumes, one in each hand, "I come laden with witnesses to prove I am right and you wrong, when you oppose my wish to sink capital in the purchase of a large dwelling, to begin in and to expand in."

The face that confronted them was of Scotch type, high cheek-bones, and too much breadth between the eyes to be lovely in form; but the depth and purity of expression in the large eyes, the expansive forehead, the well-formed nose and chin, above all the tender sensitiveness of the rich, full lips gave it attractions far superior to the charm of mere prettiness. The head was massive and well proportioned, and the auburn hair simply brushed back and showing a small, white, delicately formed ear, was fastened in a thick coil above the nape of the neck.

"'Veni, vidi, vici,' Miss Margaret," exclaimed Mons. Martin, "of course that is your motto; you have only to appear for conquest; what do you want with witnesses?"

"I want you to be serious, Mons. Martin," the girl replied smilingly, "and not in any of your frivolous or ferocious moods. Now listen:" and she raised a finger warningly and opened a volume.

"'I have seven thousand pounds in what we call the

Funds, or founded things, but I am not comfortable about the founding of them!' C'est moi," with a glance at her auditors; "and I wonder who could be comfortable with a heart to feel the *con*founded effects, as they fall upon our toiling millions." She resumed reading. "'All that I can see of them is a square bit of paper, with some ugly printing on it; and all that I know of them is that this bit of paper gives me a right to tax you';"—she again looked up. "Mr. Ruskin is addressing the working classes—you know, this," with a wave of the book, "is his 'Fors Clavigira': 'to tax you every year, and make you pay me two hundred pounds out of your wages; which is very pleasant for me.' "No, no, Mr. Ruskin," Margaret here interpolated, "it is not pleasant for us any more than for them; 'but how long will you be pleased to do so?' Ah! how long indeed?" and she dropped the volume on the table and vigorously addressed Mons. Martin: "You, revolutionist as you are, who desire and expect to overturn everything, you dare to bid me leave my money in the Funds, and refrain from a purchase which would at least free it and free my soul from chronic action of an unjust nature!"

"The Funds, Miss Margaret!" said Mons. Martin with a mocking voice, although his face looked grave; "when our revolution comes, the Funds will be swept away! so your delicate conscience may be easy."

"It is not easy," cried the girl, interrupting him, not rudely, but with the freedom of friendly confidence, "and I don't see how it should be. The revolution may never come, at least in my day, and in any case, ought we not to act at once, in accordance with the new truth we perceive? The old political economy is, so far, dead for me; I no longer think that by saving upon my expenditure I

E

increase the wage-fund, and through it, advance national progress. I belong to the new school that sees farther than that; and my conscience is *not* easy till my actions proclaim the fact."

"Ah! Miss Margaret" said her opponent, "beware less défauts of your sex! For philosophy, it is too precise, too fussy," with a smile, "if I may so say about the matters that are small. Now, look here, my child, you sell out of the Funds, some one else buys in, and assumes the very right to tax the proletariat which you so heroically resign!"

Tears sprang into Margaret's eyes, which she lowered, and as a wave of depression passed down her frame, she seated herself at Miss José's side and placed her feet on the footstool; then addressing her: "Why is it never possible to put things right? Oh, cursed spite! that I was born a parasite," she murmured in a low voice.

Instantly a small hand, wrinkled, but shapely and full of character, touched hers and a voice of exquisite timbre said: "You were born, dear, to accomplish something towards the right, although personal achievement will always seem small to the soul of lofty and wide aspiration."

The little hand was raised to Margaret's lips as she again turned to Mons. Martin and cried out a little reproachfully:

"But that other who buys into the Funds seeks interest for his money in any case. It makes no difference that he buys what I sell! All the same, I am really and truly withdrawing *my* money from making interest—that is taxing the poor;—and see here: if I buy that large house at Peterloo, and work for my daily bread with these hands," and she flourished her fair fingers with a little triumphant gesture, "surely I am no longer a parasite of the classes, but a toiling unit among the masses?"

A delicate touch of irony played on Mons. Martin's lips as, glancing over her costume and taking daintily a fold of the skirt between his first finger and thumb, he remarked :

"The toiling masses are not æsthetic, Miss Margaret; this texture is not quite the thing for the kitchen or washtub. But perhaps your toil is to be of the head? You might write," and he said this with a merry twinkle in his eye, "a treatise on your new Political Economy; but alas! even in the present system of things, the writing of books, as I know to my cost," and here he became very grave, "does not pay." Margaret had moved slightly and twitched the silk from his fingers; then, looking up with a playful expression :

"I do *not* propose to work with my head, Mons. Martin," she said; "at least that," and she nodded her head significantly, "will be gratis—into the bargain—you know."

"My silks and satins will all disappear. I will put on sackcloth, to please you, but not the ashes. I will serve you your soup in a ravissante garb of calico! There, now, you will see! But come, be serious and give us your advice. I suppose, dear," and she turned to Miss José, whilst Mons. Martin brought forward a chair and seated himself with an elaborate air of docile obedience, "you have told him all about the large house at Peterloo, and shown him Mr. Ferrier's letter?"

"Well, here," as Miss José made an affirmative sign, "is another letter"—she drew one from her pocket and unfolded it, "on the same subject. It is from Mr. Ray, jun., and," reading from the sheet in her hand, "he says:

"'My father has gone carefully over the house which is for sale at Peterloo, and for which, it appears, one offer, at

E—2

least, has already been made. It would be large enough
to accommodate a community of fifty persons or more,
and is in thorough repair from top to bottom.'

" 'It was a Nunnery, and nuns are always, my father
says, admirable tenants of whom to become the
successors.'

" 'Mr. Ferrier, I understand, has written to you and
described the building in every particular. My opinion
coincides with his, that the purchase of this house,
although, commercially speaking, the property is a great
bargain, the upset price being below its value, would be
unwise on the part of a group of individuals whose means
are small, with the single exception of your own.'

" 'Miss Karrattray and I have personally the strongest
objections to taking part in an experiment which begins
by incurring debt; but we do not shrink, as it seems to
me Mr. Ferrier does, from the possibility of a rapid
increase in the numbers of our Unitary Home; and I am
bound to tell you that my father considers its success will
be proportional to this increase. He thinks, therefore,
that if this large dwelling can be secured on the terms
spoken of by Mr. Ferrier, viz., that you purchase the
whole, but require rent from the Community for only
that portion which the Commune inhabits, the rent
rising as the numbers increase, it will place the experiment on a more secure footing, and prove highly ad-
vantageous. He bids me say that if you so decide, an
offer should be sent in without delay. I trust your friend,
Miss José, and yourself are well. My marriage with Miss
Karrattray is fixed for the tenth of next month, and Mr.
Ferrier's marriage takes place on the first.

" Believe me, yours faithfully,

" FRANCIS RAY."

Margaret placed the letter on her lap, and looked at Mons. Martin, who said gravely :

" And if the experiment should fail ? "

" If it did, Mons. Martin," the girl replied, " I should be poorer, no doubt, but, surely happier, in that I had voluntarily resigned my legal and immoral liberty, to levy toll upon my fellow-creatures. But, why should it fail ? It must not fail. Ah ! that reminds me, dear," and she turned to Miss José. " I have brought for you, at last, the history of Brook Farm ;" then lifting from the table the second of the two volumes which she had brought into the room, she nodded gaily to Mons. Martin, and added, " My second witness, you know."

Miss José took the book, and read out its title, " George Ripley ; by O. B. Frothingham. American Men of Letters ; " then returned it to Margaret, who, saying gently : " It is a strangely pathetic history," fluttered the leaves till she reached page 193, and paused.

" Ah ! here it is," she exclaimed. " Here is the point for us to take note of. 'The crushing difficulties,'" quoting from the book, "'were financial; these pressed more and more heavily month by month, and at length could not be breasted. The catastrophe came from this quarter.'" Glancing backwards along the lines, she again read aloud, "'Such obstacles might have been overcome by capital.'" Then turning back still another leaf, she resumed—"'Mankind are repelled as by an instinct, from such undertakings.—Capital avoids them. Practical ability shuns them.' "Not now, Mr. Frothingham, not now, thank goodness." Margaret commented on her text, and with a quick glance to Mons. Martin, "I don't claim to have practical ability, you know; but I have the capital, if only you will let me use it." Then again turning to the book, and citing the next passage, "'The world, no doubt, is selfish; but, so long as it is providentially so, so long as selfishness is one of the stubborn conditions of advance in righteousness, to complain of it is idle.' "Bah!" cried Margaret, closing the book. "Your climax, Mr. Frothingham, is bathos! twaddle! To complain is idle? cela va sans dire. But the indirect proposition of this passage I deny, I repudiate. Selfishness is no longer providential, in the sense of being a stubborn condition of advance. It is altruism, not selfishness that is that condition, and we are bound to make desperate efforts to produce the altruistic humanity that is required."

"Bravo! Miss Margaret," cried Mons. Martin. "Bravo! You become oratorical, to add to your other charms, and I admit the force of your reasoning; but what does Thérèse say?"

Both turned to their companion, and perceived that her mind was a little, what she would have termed, distrait.

But she spoke instantly, addressing Margaret:

"I am thinking, my dear, of another question than that of finance. It is the question of expansion, of increase in numbers that disturbs me. You see, Mr. Ferrier is one who will throw obstacles in the way; and no doubt, even amongst our present small number, there will be others, not true Socialists, but only half-hearted ones. Ah! Margaret! we shall not have our difficulties to seek, or to make. Still,"— and she looked at the girl affectionately, and reflectively, as though taking stock of commodities in the light of some commercial enterprise, "there is youth, health, culture—that is intelligence, and sentiment abreast of the age—upon our side. It is not as though my feebleness were the criterion of the Unitary Home."

Then, with a fixed gaze into futurity, not vacancy, she added, giving a little assured jerk with her chin:

"Yes, yes ; our bark will steer safely through the sand-banks of this transition epoch ; and sail out into the ocean of boundless life, although these old eyes—" and she momentarily shut them "be for ever closed before that time arrives."

"Already Margaret, we shall be obliged, you and I, to consider seriously as to numbers ; for my good landlady stands at the door of our Commune, an applicant for admission, with no correct ideas, I fear, on the difference between Mrs. Plimsoll, a communist, and Mrs. Plimsoll, mistress of her home in Primrose Bank Terrace."

Margaret smiled brightly, but Mons. Martin started to his feet, and from his pocket drew forth a cigar-case.

"Well, ladies," said he, "with Mrs. Plimsoll on the tapis, I may be permitted, I think, to retire. This weed, Miss Margaret, will sharpen the wits I am called upon to use in your service. I will meditate your problems of principle and practice ; your altruism versus selfishness ; your transposition of capital from the Funds to the infant Commune at Peterloo, of which you propose to become— nursing mother."

"Go ! go ! Mons. Martin," responded Margaret ; "go, smoke, in peace, your cigar of dreamy inactivity. That policy of yours, expecting everything, doing nothing ! I have overturned it. I have confuted you, and confounded you, by the mouth of two witnesses ; " and she flourished her two volumes as, with assumed dignity, she waved him out of the room ; then quickly turning, and seating herself by Miss José: " Now, dear," she said. " tell me all about Mrs. Plimsoll."

The smoker walked slowly up the Terrace, and rounded the corner. His reflections, at first, were pleasurable. A charming girl, that, he thought, earnest yet gay ; full of theories, yet practical, spirituelle—a rare combination. Why is she not married ? Ma foi, if I were only Englisl , and some eight years younger! The British men are either stupid pedants, or clownish; they want flesh and colour ; the spirituelle is not to their taste. Poor child ! By simple motherhood she would accomplish more for the race than by this regenerative scheme of hers. Ma foi ! and the smoke of his cigar ascended in a lively manner as though thrown off from an irritable surface.

The ladies he had left were in deep consultation. Margaret's playfulness had entirely disappeared.

" It is not the boys," Miss José was saying. " If they continue to develop, as they are doing now, we have nothing to fear from them. Careful training on our part will bring them to a high standard. They will not disgrace an altruistic cultured society. But the mother—is adaptation possible there ? You know, dear, Mrs. Plimsoll's peculiar characteristic? She is full of class prejudice, and because circumstances have thrown her out of the social circle to which she considers herself to belong, she is perpetually pluming her feathers, and calling attention to her birth, and her husband's birth, as though these phenomena gave personal distinction, and created personal merit ! The recognition of this imaginary merit is what her mind is constantly seeking. She approaches her fellow-creatures, not frankly and freely, but, with a mental attitude curiously subservient and suspicious; and if not speedily assured of their respect, she sets up her back: you know what that means ? "

" But why, then, admit her to our Unitary Home ?" said Margaret. " Let us merely take upon ourselves the education of the boys, and persuade Mrs. Plimsoll to remove to Peterloo, and live near us."

Miss José shook her head. " That, " she said firmly, would be a compromise unworthy the humanitarian order of life which we, Margaret, are aspiring to organise. Consider, love ! to make George and Harry true sons of the commune—and they are fine material, as I said ; they will mould to the form we desire ;—and to leave their mother outside, without effort on our part to give her the sentiments which we hope and believe will dominate her sons' lives ! No ! no ! such action would be a deliberate weakening of the family bond ; the contemptuous treatment of maternal and filial relations--precisely one of the great evils we deplore in the present bad system of things ! Mrs. Plimsoll too, is worthy of respect on her own merits, though not on the ground she sets forth. But here is the difficulty. Our associated members ought to know the individual idiosyncrasies, so far as I can tell them, before deciding the question, either in favour of or against her admission ; and Mrs. Plimsoll is impatient, she presses for an immediate answer. Her future, poor thing."——

" *That* difficulty, dear," cried Margaret interrupting, "need not disturb you, surely ! I will go to-morrow, if you like, to Liverpool. What is a journey to me ? I will interview all our members without delay. Mrs. Plimsoll shall not be kept long in suspense."

Miss José looked fondly at Margaret, and with paper and pencil the two proceeded to note down carefully the important points of this new and delicate mission. Miss José was the last descendant of a very ancient French family, originally royalist, and at one time immensely

wealthy. The branch of the family to which she belonged
had, however, early become republican, and her parents,
driven from France at the period of the first Empire and
deprived of fortune, had settled in England and lived
precariously, enduring many hardships with all the
stoicism and dignity that noble breeding engenders.

Their only child was carefully educated by themselves,
and launched upon the career of governess in private
families.

"The English, my Thérèse" had been said to her by
her beloved father, "are vulgarising themselves and
hurting their national life by a false system of education
in large public schools and larger day schools for boys;
large boarding schools for girls! Your life-work can only
be a tiny stream of counteracting tendency; yet, do your
best, my child, to show them that home education and
personal training has its superior advantages."

Thirty-seven years of strenuous, conscientious labour
took the vitality out of Miss José. It was a "tired
governess," indeed, that crept into the little lodging at
Primrose Bank Terrace and felt ready to lie down and die.
She had chosen Leeds because her favourite pupil lived
there, but, in six months time the girl was engaged, and
in a few weeks more had left England, to settle in a distant
home, from whence an occasional greeting, a hurried note,
full of herself, her husband, and by and by her babes, was
all that ever came to cheer the old governess who had
exhausted the best powers of her mind and heart in doing
the girl an incalculable service.

"My father, was wrong" Miss José said to herself, after
her many years of dearly-bought experience. "The
English home is not what he thought it. Within its
narrow bounds, in an atmosphere of class prejudice,

dominancy, sometimes selfishness and pride, a noble or altruistic humanity can scarcely be reared. The home itself must evolve. It must take on some new form ere it will fulfil its obligation to the youth of each generation, elevating it emotionally, educating it intellectually, and training it to virtuous habits of innocent, happy life."

Her own life had settled into a groove of peaceful, but oppressive stillness. The tiny income from her hard-won savings sufficed for her modest wants; and the prospect before her was one of old age in a lonely corner, of a sunless existence growing grayer and grayer as it waned in the gloom of approaching night.

The one human link that kept her in touch with the wide world lying around was Henri Martin's friendship. His parents had been her parent's warmest friends, and from the moment that the old people were all swept away, he had become to her as a beloved young brother. Their correspondence had been frank, confidential, regular for many years, and they met at intervals, though not frequently.

Only once in the five years of her retirement had Miss José taken a journey, and, strange to say, it was in the depth of winter. To investigate some facts concerning a family, she was making personal sacrifices to assist to emigrate, she travelled to Edinburgh, and in returning thence the incident befell which has already been related.

The misfortune of a night in the snow was the making of a fortune to her, she liked often to say. It embellished her poor life with the wealth of Margaret's love and sympathy and *gratitude,* for Miss José became her true teacher in the philosophy which every being craves who has the intellect and soul to desire harmony, consistency, unity, in human life.

"Come and live with me, dear Miss José," Margaret had said, after a year of close intercourse. "Why are you here and I there, when we love each other so much?" And Miss José had replied, "Oh, no, dear! No! Leave me the independence I have toiled for through life. It is loneliness, I grant; but, the homeliness of social equality, at least, is here. Mrs. Plimsoll's service has become the service of love. In your home of luxury, Margaret, what should I be to your servants? To your acquaintances, what? Ah!" with a shiver, "don't ask me, dear! If Communal life amongst the refined were possible, all on a footing of perfect equality and none with an atom of the de haut en bas spirit, then I might. But, no, don't let us waste emotion in vainly longing for the impossible."

Margaret cried bitterly that night in the solitude of her luxurious home. "What is my fortune to me?" she said to herself. "It will not purchase the things I care for! If I had no money, she would let me be with her always, and wait upon her, as I long to do, till her dear head is laid in the grave. I hate my money; I wish it were put, as somebody wished the poor Irish were put, 'compendiously under the sea.' To amass it, gave my father the misery of an overwrought brain; to possess it, gives me the misery of idleness, and even worse than that, the horror of feeling suspicious of my fellow-creatures."

It was true that Margaret's frankness of nature had been checked by the discovery of how her pleasant society, her divine sympathy, might be sought for the sake of favours her money enabled her to bestow; and her manner to casual acquaintances, especially gentlemen, had of late become haughty and distant.

No wonder the girl brightened with vehement hope when Vera's moan reached her. A vista of a possible different life stretched suddenly before her inward eye. If only she could get her sweet little practical school-friend to marry her Joe, and bring him and her mother to try an associated home with herself and Miss José, a real, though infantile, Commune might be formed.

Margaret laughed with a child-like glee as she won Miss José's adhesion to the scheme, and since then things had gone trippingly.

Her visit to the Wards, followed by Joe's slow, half-unwilling consent; the cordial, happy assent of the two Rays, and Rose Karrattray, and the eager offer of Isaac Spiers to join the Community: "why, it is a marching to victory!" cried Margaret. But now there had entered the field a recruit requiring caution, and Miss Jose's counsels were resumed at the station, when Margaret, next morning, was starting for Liverpool. "Put strongly, my love, the forbearance that all will have to exercise towards Mrs. Plimsoll, until she knows our members and trusts them. Then her valuable traits will appear; and the boys! It is worth some effort, indeed, to save these fine boys from ruin. Mr. Ray and Mr. Spiers will know what pitfalls and snares lie in wait for young lads with only a mother, and not a very wise one, to guide them.

"Only think, dear! This morning I heard George asking his mother for a penny to buy buns in the cricket field. She drew from her pocket two half-pennies, and George demurred 'Oh, mother, the fellows will chaff,' said he; 'they'll think me hard-up to pay with two half-pennies.'" Margaret laughed; Miss José remarked, "She did not laugh, I assure you; she approved the boy's sentiment, and searched for a penny to give him, saying,

'That's right, George; don't let the boys think us hard up!'"

Margaret's eyes sparkled with emotion as she kissed her friend, and said energetically, "These boys are charming. We *must* have them, to train them to ideas that are true and not false. Never fear, dear, they will be our boys yet," and she passed lightly into the carriage, from whence, as the train steamed forth, she signalled a loving adieu.

CHAPTER VI.

NAME, CONSTITUTION, AND FINANCE.

IT has often been thought and said that if the castles of former days—those fine old ruins that dot the country—were endowed with the human faculties of memory and speech, no tale of man's devising could compare for pathos with the entrancing histories their old walls would relate. What panoramas have they not witnessed of human life! The rise and fall of generation after generation; scenes of resplendent pomp and show, transposed by some heartrending spectacle of warlike devastation; acts of heroic nobleness and dignity; deeds of dastardly duplicity; emotions that have raised mankind above the brute; and passions, yielded to, that have debased him; and everywhere the human heart, its loves and joys, its pains and griefs, imprinted on the page of history.

But it is not alone these ancient ruins that may a tale unfold.

So rapid has movement become, during the last hundred years, in industrial and economic life and in society, that many a modern dwelling might speak to us of all the varied phases of fickle fortune, the keen vicissitudes of human life.

63

The large house at Peterloo, of which Margaret Dunmore had become owner, was built for the private residence of a man of fortune. The man or the fortune, which of the two, it does not concern us to inquire, disappeared; and the dwelling was transformed into that hybrid outcome of modern society, a Hydropathic Establishment.

It too, in its turn, proved ephemeral. The incongruous groups that set up transitorily a makebelieve home life within its walls finally departed, and a transformation scene was again enacted. A high wall was now erected upon every side of the pleasure ground, and behind it, existence was stately, formal, antiquated. One sex only was admitted into the precincts, and pale nuns with tender hearts strove to secure beneath the shelter of its roof a holy life. But that too, whether dream or reality, is not for us to say—had passed away. The dwelling remained, beautified, perhaps sanctified, by the industrial activities, the sweet aspirations of the gentle nuns who, all unconsciously, had prepared it for a new advent, a fresh departure. To make life holy was still the problem to be worked out within these walls, but, the path chosen was in every respect the converse of monastic, religious dicta.

Miss José and Margaret had removed to Peterloo, and for two months were closely engaged, with the assistance of Mr. Ray, sen., and Mr. Spiers, in superintending alterations within the dwelling and supplying the requisite furniture. Mrs. Ward, as yet in her old home in Liverpool, was consulted frequently. The newly organised brotherhood often met in her presence, and Mr. Scott, though he gave no personal adhesion, being as he said—too old a bachelor to change his ways, was an able adviser and a steady friend.

Mrs. Ward was no more exempt than formerly from physical suffering, but the weary hours were beguiled and brightened by a new interest in life, an enlarging of her mental and emotional spheres. It became to her a matter of conscience to read and think upon Socialism. Her ignorance on the subject had come home to her on every occasion on which Miss José frankly expressed her ideal of life; and Mrs. Ward was amazed to find how contact with enthusiastic and sympathetic minds, of an age and experience equal to her own, set free once more the wings of an imagination long imprisoned by personal griefs, and imparted fresh springs of vigorous vitality to the mental part that since her widowhood had pined and languished in a body of pain. After grave consultation, Mrs. Plimsoll and her boys were formally received as members of the Unitary Home, to be cherished there, and patiently borne with until transformed into genuine Communists, or until a voluntary individual request to resign the position should come from the Plimsoll side. The young widow had visited the elder one, Mrs. Ward, and met her new comrades. She had taken her measure of each as they had taken theirs of her; and on her return the remarks she let drop, with an involuntary elevation of chin, to neighbours at Primrose Bank Terrace, were to the effect that all were ladies and gentlemen of birth, and therefore would suit her! Perhaps it was gratification on this point that lifted her triumphantly to the self-sacrifice the comrades required of her. Mrs. Plimsoll had to give them a solemn pledge to resign her maternal freedom in the management of her boys. Their training and discipline must be under the authority of the Unitary Home. Again, should personal dissatisfaction arise and she desire to leave the community, she bound herself to

F

exert neither influence nor legal power over her sons, but
to let them go with her or remain, according to their own
free choice. When within two weeks of the time fixed
for removal of the Plimsoll family and furniture to Peterloo,
a sad, unexpected event occurred which led to new develop-
ments; therefore, I must relate the particulars. A half
cousin of Mrs. Plimsoll, and wife of the Rev. Walter
Cairns, died in Bradford at the birth of her third child;
and Mrs. Plimsoll immediately placed her boys in the
charge of a friend, and hastened to the aid of the bereaved
widower and newly-born infant.

Walter Cairns was a man whose delicate conscience,
when unenlightened, had been a misfortune to him: in
this sense, it had led him to make some grievous mistakes.
His early choice of the Church as a profession was a mistake, although made under a solemn sense of filial duty;
for his pious mother, having dedicated her son, from his
birth, to the Lord, naturally exerted a strong influence
over the impressionable lad to bring about what seemed
to her the fulfilment of her prayers.

His marriage was a mistake. At the age of eighteen he
was in love with a pretty face, and, in utter ignorance of
the phenomena of life, he mistook a transient passion,
indicative merely of virile manhood, for that master
passion which diffuses satisfaction throughout the entire
complexus of the civilised man, and endures to the end
of life.

His ideal of love was high. Faithfulness was insepar-
able from noble love, and since he, at the time, was truly
in love he had no hesitation in engaging to marry Miss
Napier, as soon as prudence permitted the step.

Six years of mental activity followed, and Walter
Cairns was no longer boyish, when, from his curacy in

Yorkshire, he entreated Miss Napier to resign her situation as trained nurse in the Glasgow Infirmary, and become his wife. The engagement had not been approved by the parents on either side, consequently no facilities for meeting were afforded these earnest, grave young people. On the contrary, obstacles to their attaining mutual knowledge by close intercourse were deliberately thrust in their way; and their correspondence, though regular, was not frequent.

It revealed to both discrepancies in thinking, but to neither did it ever occur as possible that the bond between them was nothing more than an echo of passion, a thing of the past. The short ten days they were together before marriage was a bitter experience, a time of agony to Walter.

That he no longer loved was plain to him, and the knowledge created self-disgust; that Miss Napier was, or would speedily become, equally indifferent to him did not reveal itself. His intelligence was, at the moment, too self-absorbed. The duty-spirit prevailed to make him false to himself and her. He thought *it was right* to fulfil the engagement; and, full of humble docility, dominated by earnest religious feeling, he took the fatal step of entering matrimony without the holy affections which alone justify and sanctify the union.

In about two years' time the conscientious strivings of husband and wife to be sympathetic in thought and feeling ceased. Both knew it was in vain, and they lived apart in all, save outward appearance.

Mrs. Cairns' narrow intellect had early matured and become rigid, no growth in ideas was possible to her; and after her first child was born, her emotions became also in a manner rigid. Their intension was great, concentrated on her

F—2

child, their expansion did not reach beyond the maternal relation—her husband was left out in the cold. To fill up his life with public interests and far-reaching thought was his resource; and the result, a very natural one, was a series of progressive changes utterly incomprehensible and appalling to his wife.

He left the English Church for a Unitarian chapel. There he gradually ceased to preach Christian doctrines. He passed into vaguer teaching, and oscillated between Theism and Pantheism till expelled by the aggrieved amongst his hearers. . . . The spring of his action at this time was the noble principle: I must be true to myself at all cost and every hazard. He hired a public hall in which to lecture, and became, to the outside world, a Free Lance, to his few earnest followers a simple inquirer after truth.

The experiment was, from the finacial standpoint, a failure. Theoretically he landed himself and his hearers in the non-Theistic or Agnostic school of thought. Pecuniarily, he landed himself, his wife, and his children (a second had been born) in penury. Spiritually, good work was done. His own soul, and the souls of a few others, were made strong in heroic devotion to truth; and the mists of doubt and delusion that obscure the incoming light of a new age were, in a little corner of the world's precious vineyard, satisfactorily cleared away.

But poor Mrs. Cairns had doubts impossible to dispel. Unable and unwilling to follow her husband's thoughts, she followed his fortunes from pillar to post with growing distrust.

Insanity, to her mind, could alone account for these changes; and when preaching was wholly resigned, and literature—a broken reed, *she* thought it to lean on—assumed as profession, she called to her side, as frequently before, her friend, counsellor, and cousin, Mrs. Plimsoll.

"Oh, Annie! my heart is broken!" she sobbed out; "the children and I, if I live—but I won't live, I know,—will starve. When baby comes, if I die, will you take it? Promise me that, Annie; for Walter, poor Walter! will soon be in an asylum."

"What nonsense!" cried Mrs. Plimsoll, cheerily. "I tell you what, Liz., you were always nervous, and now your condition . . . Why, Walter is as sane as I am, only foolish. I could have told him that Hall business would come to grief. But men will be men, surely you might know that by this time! As for starving, Walter has excellent friends, who would help him with money at once if he were not so proud. Men hate to receive favours. . . . An infidel, did you say? They call him an infidel! Who cares what they call him? We know—you and I—he is a good man, a kind husband; and as for religion, why, officers in the army, gentlemen born, the highest in the land, have, many of them, no religion. My husband always said that, and he himself—'twould puzzle me to say what *he* was! 'I was brought up a Brother,' he used to remark, when his not going to church was commented on; and, alone with me, he would laugh and say, 'Lucky for me I was born in Plymouth. These inquisitorial bigots deserve to be humbugged.'" Thus poor Mrs. Cairns' irrational fears were assuaged by Mrs. Plimsoll's equally non-rational confidence; and the former held on her martyr-like path till her third child was born, and then succumbed.

At midnight, on the 1st of November, 1890, Walter sat by the bedside of his dying wife, her hand tenderly pressed in his; and within his heart was a weight of sorrow,

an almost undue sense of the failure of their married
life.

An overwhelming wave of emotion swept over his soul
and unsealed his lips. "Lizzie!" he whispered, "dear
wife, I have wronged you—betrayed you. I ought to have
known we could not be happy together. Forgive me, dear
love." The heavy lids were raised, and eyes of bewilderment fixed on him.

Did he think, simple man, that the approach of death
reveals all life's secrets? Alas! the two minds were as far
apart as before. The light of a transcendental joy spread
over her face as Lizzie gasped weakly, "My prayers are
heard! my husband brought back to the fold of Jesus.
Oh, Walter! our children! make them Christians. . .
Cousin Annie will help." Faintness here interrupted the
broken speech. It ceased, and was never resumed.
The dawn of a new day found Walter watching by a
silent form whose heart-beats grew fainter and fainter,
till stillness prevailed in the chamber of death, and the
grief-stricken, broken man was alone with his bitter
memories.

Mrs. Plimsoll's nature is active, sanguine. She assumed
supremacy in the widower's house; met all the requirements of his children, but created a breezy atmosphere of
bustle that drove him almost distracted.

He shut himself into his study, and at the end of one
week Mrs. Plimsoll had worked out a logical inference :
If Walter were sane, he was neglecting his duties as
father; if not sane, the children could not be left with
him: ergo, she, Mrs. Plimsoll, must stay in Bradford, or
carry the whole family with her to Peterloo!

Into the study she penetrated, armed, I might call it,
with the conclusion only, the final limb of her logical

syllogism. But that was sufficient to impale Mr. Cairns on the horns of a dilemma.

To choose the less of two evils was all he could hope for, and, in a mood verging upon despair, he roused himself to travel to Peterloo, and be introduced to a posse of strangers from whom, at the moment, he really hoped for nothing.

Can my reader form any conception of the blessed experience that awaited him there?

Not so! unless he or she has trodden the winepress alone, unless he has traversed vast regions of speculative thought, and all the while longing for the touch of a kindred soul to lighten the sublime but awful solitude.

It was nothing less than the breath of a new and inspiring life that Walter Cairns inhaled in the presence of Miss José, Margaret, and Rose.

The two former were as free as himself from theological dogma, although a vital religion animated their every action. And Rose, with her childlike simplicity and her fulness of knowledge concerning those social problems to which Walter was beginning to turn his whole attention, Rose stepped into cordial sympathy at once with the desolate man, and played on the deepest strings of his sensitive nature with so delicate a touch that, behold! what she brought forth was inward music.

When Mrs. Plimsoll removed to Peterloo, her infant charge was with her; and, later by some three or four weeks, Walter Cairns,—he had dropped the reverend,— his daughter Esther, aged fifteen, and his son Percy, aged twelve, followed from Bradford, and were installed in the newly-housed community.

"*La Maison*," the new name of the communal dwelling, is carved on the front. It was chosen by the group although its suggestion arose from a little skirmish of Margaret's with Mons. Martin.

"You English have no genius for easy social life," had said Mons. Martin; "Malaise, not bien aise, characterizes even your homes! The little ones of your large families are not at ease with monsieur the papa. And —— But who is it, Miss Margaret, who is always writing about your debasing the currency? Monsieur is right. That word *home,* how you have debased it! A lady sends you an invitation to her 'at home' on such an evening, and when you go, behold! you are not at home in the least! you are in the midst of a stiff and stately *cérémonie!* Bah! You will always be a nation of workers, industrious to the core; your enjoyments are all laborious; but social, genial, flexible, never!"

Margaret combated this allegation in the playful spirit of banter that had taken possession, somehow, of her relations with Mons. Martin; nevertheless, it sank deeply into her heart.

She pondered the defects of English character, and traced them, she thought, to defects in the English home.

The remedy was not easy to see; but she would devote her life to this problem, and accomplish something, however small, in the exposure of these defects, the inauguration of a remedial system. This had become the central idea of her inmost thoughts, the pivot of her existence.

At one of the preliminary meetings of the brotherhood Margaret made a speech on this subject.

"As part of the great order of the future," said she, "our fundamental position is that of all Socialists. We hold the equal duty of all to labour; the belief that ultimately society must abolish the proletarianism of the majority, and bring the largest possible measure of the amenities of life within the reach of all. This may be called our Social Ideal our Economic Creed. But as a unit in the great order or system of the future—a socialist family or small communal group,—we have, in my view, another special aim. It is in reference to the enjoyments rather than the industries of life.

"To the motto, 'without work no enjoyment,' we should add, and emphasize if possible—and *no work without enjoyment.*

"We are often, as a nation," with a glance round, "I allude, of course, to the English, who are in a majority here, taunted with our inability to enjoy ; and the taunt has in it a measure of truth. Let us make it our special business to adapt ourselves, and all who may at any time join our number, to the enjoyment of a rich, full, harmonious, broadly social domesticity ; and pledge ourselves to promote the creation of that domesticity from day to day and hour to hour.

"Home is a word that in some ears has lost its charm. By false applications of the term we have, alas ! debased its currency. I propose, therefore, partly for that reason, partly because it is our happiness to have comrades of another race and tongue within our intended home, to substitute the French term, La Maison, and should my proposal be approved and adopted, I need only add that, personally, I will do my utmost to make all of you feel, as you cross the threshold, that you are indeed and in truth, *à la maison.*"

Having purchased La Maison with her own private fortune, Margaret grew bolder in asserting her independent, just, and generous will.

She braved the displeasure of legal counsellors and a few distant relatives, and formally made over the building to the members of the Unitary Home as a free gift for the term of its existence. If the group should cease to exist whilst Margaret still lived, she would then be entitled to resume possession of the house.

Again, should it come to an end, with Margaret dead, and the present disorganized social system still lingering, the building would be sold, and the proceeds divided equally among the separating communists.

Before the assembling of the group within the walls, which took place during the third week of November, various matters had been discussed. The questionings and doubts of individual members were brought forward and dealt with, in some cases resolved; and by each adult member a document entitled *Our Constitution* was agreed to and formally signed.

In the course of these confidential discussions it soon became evident that, of the group, only Joe Ferrier and Mrs. Plimsoll were strongly individualistic.

Self-interest made them adherents, and to get on in life, to amass property, to make the children of the Commune healthy, wealthy, and worldly-wise, ought, in their view, they frankly stated it, to be the whole business of the Unitary Home.

Even Vera, who had never formulated to herself any theory of life, here gently demurred.

" Oh, Joe ! " she remarked, " we ought not to live to ourselves alone; and although the *we* does mean a lot of people living happily together, it surely would be selfish to do nothing and care nothing for the world outside ! I mean, we should make it our business, you know, to help the poor, or do something for people who are not as well off as we are. Could we work for bazaars? or save up some money and start a 'mother's meeting' of our own?"

These simple suggestions were not adopted, but the clear-minded Collectivists in the group, viz., Mr. Spiers, Miss José, Margaret, Mr. Ray, sen., and Rose, who had earnestly thought out a scheme of noble associated life, were immensely aided by the weight thrown into the scale on their side by Vera and others, who, without thinking much on that terrible problem of how to accomplish real good in a world all torn and bleeding with conflict, yet felt all the generous impulses of full-fledged Socialism.

"The public spirit of our Unitary Home (it was finally settled) must extend to the uttermost limits of the earth.

"It is nothing less than the Happiness of all Mankind we desire, and shall strive in some small measure to promote. To this end we purpose, first, to show by our life and conduct, in what true happiness consists.

"It does not consist in wealth, luxury, idleness; therefore, we eschew all these. Our home must never be wealthy, never luxurious, never the abode of idleness.

"Within its walls abundant comfort, with simplicity, must be maintained; elegance and refinement, without show or glitter. And whoever departs from this principle, in opinion or action, will be liable to criticism in open council, or free to withdraw from the Commune.

"Our second method of promoting General Happiness is, by direct action upon the young; and here we aspire to extension of the action beyond the children of our Unitary Home. The day-school we shall carefully organize is certain to be, for months, perhaps years, very small; for around Peterloo there are not, we fear, many parents

sufficiently advanced in thought to commit their children
to our care. To the average public mind, our school will
seem non-religious. The Bible will not be used as a text-
book. We regard it as human, a venerable monument of
past ages, and although the work it has done, in evolving
the conscience of man, and aiding his progress from barbarism to civilisation is immense, we perceive that its
teaching now is discordant, confusing, partly obsolete, and
in no way harmonious with the revealed truths of a scientific age.

"We set it aside, therefore, reverently, and turn to
modern books, the highest and best we can find.

"Our teaching throughout will be primarily religious.
That is, we will not, as at most schools is done, grind the
gerund stone of ordinary routine, to turn out men and
women of fashion able only, and certainly willing, to live
on the labour of others: scholarly, otiose pedants: keen
sharpers, or what, by a curious irony, are called 'business
men,' though their business is not to produce wealth, but
simply to manipulate and distribute it, whilst lining their
pockets with gold in the process: drudges able to work in
a dreary mechanical way to maintain and embellish the
lives of others, while their own individual lives are sunk
in hideous foulness, poverty, squalor!

"In contra-distinction to this, our school will take in-
finite pains to produce Humanity of a noble, superior
type—men and women eager to do useful work, and
capable of doing it intelligently, skilfully, pleasurably;
their one aim the general good, their one effort the service
of their brethren; and genial, generous love the vital
spring of action throughout life.

"Every tendency to dominancy in childhood will be carefully subdued, and the barbarous instincts—anger, re-

venge, hatred, jealousy, cunning, greed—studiously nipped in the bud. Conduct will be put before cleverness, even culture ; and happiness, not wealth, pointed out as the goal of individual effort.

"Our third method of promoting general happiness is by action upon the public.

"There will be no indiscriminate charity, however, with us ; no eleemosynary aid that, in supporting individuals, is hurtful to the race.

"We will search for the social forces that are truly remedial, and aid such. We will steadfastly bear in mind the causes of our present evil social state, and its transitional condition, and support such action as deals with these causes alone ; whilst, at the same time, we strive to enlighten the public on the principles and practical outcome of Socialism, so as to prepare for the happier future of which this transition epoch is merely the unavoidable, discordant prelude."

To launch a Socialistic experiment in transition surroundings on a basis of non-coercive solidarity,—the task is not easy !

I have to admit that the pounds, shillings, and pence question was a severe test of sincerity to those who as yet had not fully thought out their newly-adopted principles. It created earnest discussion, some heart-burning, and, even when settled, a few scruples and doubts.

The settlement was as follows :—

Whoever possessed an income, whether from land, saved capital, or individual labour, became bound to yield two-thirds of the same to the Community, retaining one-third for his or her own private use. Thus, Mrs. Ward's annual income of £600 per annum yielded £400 for the general expenses, and £200 for individual expenditure ; while

Miss José, whose life-long toil had secured to her only £80 a year, threw into the general purse £53 6s. 8d., and Vera brought nothing at all save personal services.

The possession of money is simply an accident of birth, or outward condition, and must not directly affect the acceptance or rejection of candidates for the Unitary Home. The requisite possessions are inward, not outward, viz., a gentle, sympathetic nature, and qualifications for becoming a worker. The work of each would depend partly on personal choice, but subject to the determining will of the group. The income of the group, from whatever source received, must be kept steadily at a point that will easily cover the expenses of a comfortable, elegant, secure home; and this, while maintaining a sufficient staff of workers within doors, may necessitate the finding of remunerative work for many members outside, or may, on the other hand, set some of the workers free to engage in unremunerative public service on the lines already laid down.

Margaret's fortune, notwithstanding the purchase of La Maison, gave an income as nearly as could be computed of £1,840 per annum. Two-thirds of that sum, viz., £1,226 13s. 4d., made a strong backbone for the yearly income, and Margaret rejoiced to think that, in contrast to poor Brook Farm, the " crushing difficulties " that might lie in the path of La Maison were not likely to prove " financial." Already three members as penniless as Vera had been welcomed under its roof—Rose, now Mrs. Francis Ray, her young sister Lucy, aged sixteen, and Dr. Basil Karrattray.

Lucy was destined for self-support as early as possible, and the feeble mother in Devonshire scanned advertisement lists for a nursery-governess crevice in the unsocia social ring with a pain at the heart born of timid fears for her innocent darling's happiness.

To her the relief was incalculable when Mrs. Ward proposed to receive her on trial for a month, previous to the opening of the Unitary Home, in which, should mutual satisfaction result from the visit, she would be cherished as a daughter, her further development promoted and guided, and her activities directed to the special function of giving such personal services as chronic invalidism imperatively requires.

Dr. Basil was still within the Rectory, like a vessel in port with a broken shaft! To bring the figure nearer the fact, however, one must think of the vessel straining to leave the port, panting and blowing with self-generated steam, while, alas! utterly disabled.

Like Walter Cairns, his passionate youth had culminated in a marriage engagement, and, behold, at twenty-seven, when he ought, one would think, to be within reach of the world's goal in the race of life, viz., self dependence and marriage, he is tied hand and foot at the starting point!

Rose's marriage brought him into contact with Vera, Margaret, Joe Ferrier, and Mr. Ray; and what resulted therefrom was cordial hands outstretched to draw him into La Maison—a new haven of refuge from whence he, in thorough repair, might once more make or not, as time alone would reveal, canvas flying, for the open sea.

Meanwhile, for restoration of health, mental activity and a sphere for the same must be found. La Maison must have a Laboratory. The library must be furnished with the most recent books on medical science. The young doctor will study to keep his knowledge abreast of the times; he will practise if opportunity occurs; he will teach such science as he is familiar with to such scholars as may appear ; he will act as guardian and guide to the inmates of his home in all matters relating to sanitation or health.

The Plimsoll income was small, nothing more than the Government annuity of a captain's widow, and the pittance for the boys from the same source.

Walter Cairns' private income was no larger. But with Mr. Spiers, Mr. Ray, Frank, and Mons. Martin's means added in the ratio above described, the Finance Committee might reckon on resources amounting to about two thousand two hundred pounds per annum.

CHAPTER VII.

LA MAISON.

La Maison covers a considerable area, and consists of a ground-floor with two stories above.

Beneath the ground-floor there are cellars and storerooms, but no inhabited chambers. The ground floor is appropriated to purposes of education, culture, amusement, and public service; and the first floor to domesticity. It is here that the nursery is placed, some parlours also, where privacy can be secured by a simple request for non-intrusion affixed outside the door; and the salon, where domestic social evenings are spent.

To the upper story is relegated the eating and drinking, the cooking and stewing, the baking and brewing; in short, all that appertains to preparing and disposing of food.

This departure from ordinary custom in private dwellings is no mere outcome of whimsical eccentricity. It is better, so, had been the decision of minds that examined the subject under three different aspects, viz., the sanitary or healthful, the æsthetic, and the educational. On the latter Miss José had spoken with verve, and there shone at the moment from the eyes of the childless old maid the light of maternal wisdom and the warmth of maternal love.

81   G

"Our children," said she, "must learn, without effort, to subordinate physical appetites to the higher enjoyments of an intellectual, emotional existence. In ordinary society the pleasures of the table are coarsely intermixed with social pleasures of every kind; and the young of a race entrammelled, as yet, in the relics of its barbaric stage, get no aid whatever in a vital point of education, viz., the distinguishing between gratifications that are voluptuous, carnal, and those that, though sensuous still, are ennobling and elevating in the highest degree."

"Is this remark," inquired Joe, with a slightly supercilious tone, "apropos of our kitchen? do you, or does any one, suppose that the English would care less for eating and drinking if their kitchens were all consigned to their garrets?"

Henri Martin interposed. "Not so fast, my good fellow. Let us get at our theories, our principles of action, before we arrive at *que faire.* As I understand her, Miss José desires that our household arrangements should indicate our principles, and in this matter of alimentation these should point to the fact that the eating and drinking in our Unitary Home is a necessity of living, but by no means the predominant business of life."

"I entirely agree with Miss José on this subject," said Mrs. Ward. "I remember when I was a child---I was educated at home—the atmosphere of the house, when a dinner party was about to take place, developed my gustatory sense in no ordinary degree. The kitchen, dining-room, and school-room were on one floor; savoury odours reached my nose, a bustle of preparation excited my nerves; I caught glimpses of fruit and flowers, and glittering silver and glass, till my imagination was all aglow. Its images were neither simple nor healthy. I thought of myself as a lady in fairy-like, gorgeous attire, and feasting unchidden on dainties and sweets to the brim of my childish desire!

"I certainly think that in training our children to right ideas of life we shall gain much by placing our refectory and kitchen upstairs; and I trust that dinner parties and exceptional feasting of every kind will be eschewed by us. Of course we shall be hospitable. Guests will be warmly welcomed; good and abundant food liberally supplied; but as for banqueting, sumptuous feeding, let us, dear friends, have none of it.

"I betray no confidence when I tell you of a beloved friend's painful experience, for she herself desires that the practical lessons of her life may serve to guide others. She married young, and, in utter ignorance of the fact that her husband was a martyr to that morbid irresistible craving for stimulants which is, alas! the ruin of tens of thousands in this land. How had he fallen victim to the fatal malady that wrecked their married happiness? The gentle wife pondered that question, and one day drew from her husband an artless, to her appalling, revelation. 'My father,' said he, 'was a hospitable man; he kept an excellent cellar, and often entertained his friends. The butler and I together drained the wine-glasses after every dinner party! You see, I was a lonely boy, not yet in my teens. My father had married for the second time; my step-mother's babes were in the nursery. The butler was my greatest friend, I grew to love wine as he did ——'"

No comments were made on Mrs. Ward's tale; but the decision reached by the comrades was this: Since our school must be on the lower level, our eating shall be on the upper.

It may, or may not, affect our children's minds, but in

G—2

every domestic arrangement the contingency of a possible action, favourable or otherwise, on the training of youth, must be foreseen and taken into account.

We are banded together to live a life that will tell upon our children's children, to untold generations. No action is trivial in view of so momentous an issue. Deliberately we apply to ourselves the lines :—

> " Fathers, leading in life's hard road,
>   Be sure of the steps you take ;
> Then the sons you love, when grey-haired men,
>   Will tread in them for your sake.
> When grey-haired men to *their* sons will say :
>   We tread in our fathers' steps to-day."

The inconveniences of a kitchen at the top of a house were carefully considered.

Meat-safes were specially adapted for, and placed upon, the roof; and an elevator, also outside, conveys, to the ladies' hands, all supplies from below, without toilsome porterage by way of the staircase.

The spacious scullery has every appliance for work, on modern methods.

The floor, on which stands the plate racks, slopes into a sink, which renders drying unnecessary. Small mops are provided for washing dishes, and waterproof gloves for paring potatoes and cleansing vegetables. Consequently, delicate hands engaged there from day to day neither stain nor become coarse and ugly.

To facilitate service at table, the large refectory is next to the kitchen, and a service window between precludes all burdensome carrying of cooked meats to and fro.

With the one exception of afternoon tea—which every adult member is at liberty to serve in, or carry to his own room, or to salon or parlour, as he may choose—all meals are served in the refectory, and members in health must partake of them there.

The children have dinner at the luncheon hour, and their evening meal an hour and a-half before the late dinner at seven. The cup of coffee, which all who desire it find placed in the refectory at eight o'clock, concludes the alimentation for the day.

The food material, its quality and manner of treatment and presentation, created discussion.

Old Mr. Ray has prejudices here that bias his usually sound judgment. He hates entremets of every kind! He calls them French kickshaws, and thinks them accountable, in some mysterious way, for the corruption he deplores in general society! The remedial efficacy of primitive habits and customs is what he believes in; and gravely did he exhort his comrades to make oatmeal porridge the chief part of the children's diet, and, in their own, to give due prominence to the worthy roast beef of Old England.

"But, dear Mr. Ray," cried Margaret, "John Bull is no longer what he was! The creature is changed. Differentiation has taken place throughout his entire economy. His digestive apparatus, his palate and appetite, are moulded to the complexities of civilisation, and is it not simply our duty to provide such food as these complexities demand? In this matter, no doubt, all are not alike. Surely we should strive to suit all! Your porridge for breakfast must not be forgotten; but, Mons. Martin! why, I believe he would choke if we fed him on roasts, and rounds and underdone steaks!"

"Not shoke, Miss Margaret," Mons. Martin interpolated in a low tone, "but shock; I would be shock; I would run away."

" For my own part," said Vera, sweetly, "I care not what I eat. I could live the year round on cold mutton and rice pudding, but dear mother's appetite is small and dainty ;—and Joe! Oh! I shall be sorry if our dinners must always be plain. I wished so to learn how to cook all the sweets he enjoys, and the Yorkshire pudding." ...

Dr. Basil spoke next, from the scientific standpoint of health requirements; Miss José followed from the standpoint or educational requirements; and Mr. Spiers summed up on the basis of economic considerations.

The result was as follows : Variety in food is a sine quâ non, and also scrupulous neatness, cleanness and freshness in table appointments.

But simplicity, the absence of useless conventions and expensive equipments, will be studied at every point.

No solid silver or finely-cut crystal will be used in the Unitary Home. They are over costly, and their preservation creates unnecessary anxiety and care. The electroplate is kept brilliant by a simple method. At each washing after meals the ladies have by them a vessel filled with moist whitening. Into this, from hot water, they straightway plunge each fork and spoon, and leave them there till the process of cleansing tea-cups, etc., is completed, when, removing the plate from its earthy bed, the deft use of a dry towel and chamois-leather causes it to responsively shine.

The waiting at table was a problem that strangely simplified itself when tested by practice. Order and quietness are indispensable during meals, that conversation may have free play. Is elaborate waiting, then, necessary ?

It was tried, but speedily relinquished !

At dinner, which always embraces three courses, the

third, as a rule, being fruit, the first and third are placed on the table before the household is seated.

The second course stands on a hot-plate on the inner side, and a table on the dining-room side of the service window.

The necessary condiments and vegetables are within reach of each diner; the plates are passed quietly from hand to hand; and at the end of the course, a lady and gentleman, told off for this service, rise from table and make the various changes required.

At luncheon some of the men are absent; the children are present. The same order and repose are skilfully maintained, and the utmost attention is paid to training the young in habits of delicate propriety, of gentle, refined deportment at table.

The instinctive craving for sweets and acids in children is lavishly gratified. Apples and sugar they can have without restriction, whilst unwholesome confections they do not at any time see.

The household labours of a manual kind fall naturally into three divisions: first, all that appertains to food; second, what relates to comfort, cleanliness, health within doors; third, the tendance of children and invalids.

Washing and dressing of linen for the entire household is consigned to the nearest steam-laundry.

The group is at present too small to warrant the introduction of costly steam-washing appliances under the roof of the Unitary Home; yet the comrades are bound, in principle, to avail themselves of every discovery in practical science that lightens the necessary labours of man.

Of the three divisions, the second, whilst widest, is perhaps the least attractive.

To repair household linen, lift carpets and rugs, and

with duster and broom, a sharp eye and apt fingers, to establish and maintain, throughout the whole dwelling, order and cleanliness—the function is not easy! To Lucy, in anticipation, it was simply repulsive!

"Oh! dear Mrs. Ward!" she cried, before entering La Maison, "I will not be one of the housemaids, please! Please remember that! I will wait upon you hand and foot; I will nurse that dear baby Mrs. Plimsoll is to bring; I will cook, if you like; but the dirty housework! oh! pray," with a shudder, "do not ask me!"

Youth is happily plastic, and Lucy's prejudices melted away in a sunshine of elevated thought and feeling. To let no one be selfish, or even fastidious, in choice of her occupation—this was a mood of mind that Lucy unconsciously learned. Another home-lesson was this: we must socialize our domestic work, we must make all our members skilful, intelligent factors in the ways and means of existence. In a few weeks' time it became Lucy's ambition to understand the entire domestic menage, to fit herself conscientiously to aid it, when need be, at any or each individual point.

The system adopted to carry out the principle that labour should not be mechanical merely—that workers are not to be hands, in the technical sense, but workers of wit, applying their minds to each domestic duty with the keen enjoyment of intellect and practical power devoted to serviceable uses,—the system adopted is as follows. An executive committee, consisting of two male and wo female members—elected by ballot at the end of each six months,—meets every evening, to arrange the work of the following day, and appoint the members required to perform the work.

Ten minutes, as a rule, suffices for this duty. A copy

of the appointments is quickly written out, and hung in a prominent position for the members' inspection.

To vary employment, especially in the case of the young, is distinctly aimed at; and, instead of weary monotony, a breeze of healthful activity and excitement pervades the household.

The healing efficacy of this household atmosphere has been put to the test in one instance—that of Ruth Amor, a girl whose history my reader will learn in the next chapter. When she entered the Unitary Home the spring of her life seemed broken; her hope, her trust in mankind were wellnigh gone. She was an instrument tuned by Nature to happiness, whose strings had been roughly jarred, almost shattered, the music changed to discords, to pitiful wailings. To mope in La Maison is simply impossible! Life, with its varied duties, its brisk occupations, and love as varied, solicit Ruth's faculties —mental, moral, emotional.

The tender regard of the motherly women, the manly respect of the brotherhood, the spasmodic effusions of Vera's and Lucy's affection, the boisterous demonstrations of the boys, and, above all, the clinging touch of the helpless infant—these were curative agencies playing with ethereal delicacy on the sensitive wounds of the broken heart, and in four short months from the day of her entrance, Ruth Amor found in La Maison, her home.

In these first four months she was simply a probationer. At the end of that time she assumed with joyful alacrity the responsibilities of a member, and joined the General Council.

That council embraces all adult associates.

The duties are, to settle all questions relating to the general interests, or appoint a committee to do so, and also to give decision in matters of dispute that arise from time to time in the special committees.

Of these there are four, in addition to the Executive Committee.

There is first, a Finance Committee; second, an Amusement Committee; third, an Education Committee; and fourth, a Public Service Committee.

"It's muckle cry, an' little oo," was the rather caustic remark of old Mr. Ray, made in his vernacular, when these committees were organized; but to the more idealistic minds within the community their utility was by no means confined to the immediate and tangible results.

"We must train ourselves and our young people," said Mr. Spiers, "to the expression and discussion of social thought, as well as to its outcome in socialized action. From this point of view committees are invaluable. Besides, original minds must have scope for free suggestion; conservative minds must learn to dissent, on rational grounds; both will acquire habits of tolerance, of respectful regard for individual opinion, and all be alike stimulated to think about and care for the general interests of mankind with an ardent and profound public spirit."

George and Harry Plimsoll were not deemed too young to gain something from this form of training.

The sphere of amusements comes well within range of their interest, and great was their satisfaction to find their names enrolled on that committee.

"*I* will vote," said Harry, "for football every day," but George demurred, from a vague sense of injustice—the germ, though unconscious, of sympathetic feeling.

"The ladies might not like that," said he, "we should try to find out what Lucy and Vera and Esther like best, and Rose. Oh! Harry, Mrs. Rose should not run much!"

I know that. Dr. Basil said so. I won't vote for football too often."

No one in La Maison is reminded of Edgar Poe's tuneful lines on :

" The Bells—Golden Bells,
 . . . . the swinging and the ringing,
" Of the bells, bells, bells."

For, in La Maison, there are no bells, only telephones. These are liberally supplied and disposed with central connections, so that inmates of the house may readily communicate with each other from any or every part of it.

Hot air and fresh air are propelled through the passages by the newest scientific method; and in every bed-chamber the open fire-place is fitted, for consumption of coal, or for gas, according to the personal predilection of the occupant.

The lighting of the house is not done, as yet, by electricity, though the future, no doubt, gives promise of change in that direction, but by gas, with appliances for removing carbonic acid, and maintaining freshness of atmosphere within each room.

Are there any broad distinctions between masculine and feminine employments, which we, of a new order, are bound to respect ?

This question was matter of grave consideration and lively discussion on more than one occasion.

" We are deposing, man," said Margaret, " from headship in our family group. Ours is not a family despotism, as amongst Russian peasants. Stepniak tells us that in their family groups there is complete dependence of women upon the stubborn will of the elderly headman, or headmen !

" Not so with us. All the more, should not we regard functional distinctions, if any such exist, in arranging our domestic, our economic work ? "

To Mrs. Plimsoll's lips there arose the fishermen's dirge, and with childlike faith in the general fitness of her inspirations, she quoted gravely,—

" Men must work, and women must weep."

" Ah, there ! " cried Rose, " that is just what we want to see altered. We would work and weep together, would share side by side the toils and risks and joys of life, and mingle our tears in its sorrows.

" Is there any work proper to men that women may not, ought not, to share ? Women do work in fields and at coal pits—no labour is harder ; and in fever-hospitals— what position could be more dangerous ?

"Dare we say there is any real distinction that must for ever preclude close union and fellowship of the sexes in all the varied activities of life ? "

From the first, Joe Ferrier had stated distinctly that to him domestic work of every description seemed essentially feminine. He would stick to his office, his desk and pen, as much more manly. Of course he could brush his own boots if the others decided so to do ; and he would not object to rise from table and change plates, etc., with Vera; but there he meant to draw the line. If the ladies broke down in the work—and, for his part, he thought that extremely likely—he should vote for the servant element to the rescue. A modified form of the old regime.

Mr. Ray, senr., had opinions quite as pronounced, and diametrically opposite.

The pen was no more manly than the needle. A spade might be more manly, for a woman's hand and foot are scarcely adapted to wield it with proper effect. If a man liked to sit all day at a desk, why should he not like to sit at a table darning stockings ? He hated such trivial distinctions ! All work was alike to him ; if only he could do it.

He feared he was too old to learn how to cook, though he could always make his own porridge, if the sisters would allow him ; but working the elevator, attending to the stove, breaking wood, polishing floors, sweeping passages—all these he would do for the Commune, and welcome, he said in his old-fashioned way.

Outside, he intended to give all the time he could spare to the garden. He loved garden work, and would make the youngsters love it too. With their help, and Frank's, it would be queer if the table were not well supplied with garden produce.

Mons. Martin's special vocation is propagandism.

"I am opposed," says he, " to political, social, industrial tyranny in every land.

"My rôle is, to work for a complete revolution in the method of the production and distribution of wealth : to educate the working classes in Socialism by writing and public speaking.

"Our Unitary Home will be my basis of operations; I must make flying visits to London, Paris, and elsewhere ; but when here, my habits will be social, my activities socialized. If yon want me, Miss Margaret, to faire la cuisine —— "

" You shall not come into the nursery," Mrs. Plimsoll interrupted, with decision. " The baby is English." This she added as though the explanatory quality of the statement were self-evident !

The Frenchman bowed, replying flippantly : " Merci.

Madame. He is rather small for a patriot or a conspirator! think you are right, my duties do not lie there!!"——

Isaac Spiers is a man of wholly different calibre from Henri Martin. Agitation is not in his line.

Although not deficient in practical power, his special gift is able reflection. He has travelled over the world, and studied nature at first hand, reading the secrets of evolution, into no matter what form of barbarism or semi-civilisation it has moulded the various races of man. In the vast biological fields where Herbert Spencer has illumined the darkness, and ranged into order a perfect chaos of unclassified facts, Isaac Spiers has followed his footsteps: beyond that, the latter has shot ahead of his great master. In the fields of sociological facts the disciple stands pioneer.

"We are on the verge," says he, "of a new epoch: one of evolution become conscious!

"We must turn this glorious lamp, that has lighted up for us the past, upon the future.

"We must see with prophetic eye along the line. We must traverse, with broad understanding, the windings, the complex conditions of social progress.

"We must gather into our hands the reins of the steeds that hitherto have carried us whither we knew not, and compel them to carry us whither we will.

"Evolution is not yet complete. It is slowly evolving its master, its spiritual dictator—socialised man. He, with his tender heart, his right reason, his philosophical brain, he, must sooner or later guide evolution in relation to man, and enlist all controllable forces in the highest, noblest mission—the production of general happiness."

In social experiment, no man could be better guide, philosopher, or friend, than Isaac Spiers.

Although his engagement in Liverpool absorbed a portion of his time, he eagerly, on entering La Maison, devoted himself to the task of organisation. He is chairman of the General Council, and member of every Committee.

No detail of domestic experience is insignificant in his eyes. He chronicles all for guidance; and guards his associates against the repetition of blunders.

He has elaborated a system of Domestic Criticism, to be applied as necessity requires, for a threefold purpose, viz., to check tyranny and gossip; to mould individual conduct aright; and to develop character in desirable, that is, *social* directions.

He has devised a method of training children in nursery and schoolroom, a systematic discipline independent of arbitrary authority, and non-injurious to the natural spontaneity, the beautiful innocence of the free untrammelled child-nature.

But here he was ably aided by Miss José, Rose Ray, and Walter Cairns. These formed, with him, the Education Committee, and diligently have they worked, considering theories, putting them to the test, so far as was practicable, in their, as yet, very limited sphere, and sparing no pains to induce, by honest, legitimate means, other parents to place their children in charge of the Unitary Home.

A day-school is gradually forming. Dr. Basil also has already some students in the Laboratory, to whom he daily gives lessons in practical chemistry. Of these, Esther Cairns is the brightest; but we shall speak of the lasses, and what is taught there, later on.

CHAPTER VIII.

RUTH.

THE pale girl with pathetic face, who had found a refuge in La Maison, has a tragic history behind her.

That history must now be told: and, because painfully, it shall be briefly.

Five years previous to the day when Ruth entered La Maison, a widow and her two young daughters travelled up to London from the Lake district of Cumberland.

In that great centre of industry, grief might be hidden, pride ignored, and surely work, of some kind, be found, remunerative enough to keep alive the stricken trio.

The promising career of young Dr. Amor, of Ambleside, had suddenly come to an end.

Mental depression, consequent upon the collapse of an American Wood Company in which he had rashly embarked his small savings, prepared his physical system to harbour the fatal germs of disease to which his profession daily exposed him.

The fever that his patient Abel Threlkeld, peasant farmer, easily surmounted, laid hold on the doctor; and the brain-force, that in the first case supported the victim against the enemy, turned traitor to the cause when the victim became the doctor! Anxiety, worry, the delicate susceptibilities of a mobile mind ever tending to forecast the future—these all proved aids to the enemy. In ten short days the battle was over, and Mrs. Amor was husbandless, all but penniless, with Lizzie and Ruth to cherish, and, if that were possible, live for.

It seemed to her not possible, in scenes of happy days, where memory confronted her perpetually with contrasts too painful to be borne.

The cry of her heart became—" Take me away, O God; whither I care not; but into new scenes, that I may sometimes, at least, forget."

So she packed up her belongings; sold the furniture, which an ante-nuptial contract had secured to her; and, with the proceeds in her pocket, in her heart blank joylessness, but her head full of faith in her own activities and hopefulness begotten of ignorance, betook herself to London, and plunged into its abysses.

Her plan was, that the girls should find daily teaching, whilst she would accomplish the domestic work for themselves and one lodger, whose accommodation must be possible in the small suburban dwelling her means would suffice to furnish.

Does my reader know what it is to be unknown amidst numbers? To have no weight, no social position, no patronage, no lever by which to compel attention to that heart-rending prayer—Give us honest work, that we may live, and not die? A prayer that by oft-repetition has hardened the hearts of employers and turned them to stone.

Oh! you hateful system of competition, that grinds humanity to the dust! Slavery and slave-driving are the outcome of your action. The wealth ye produce may be metal, but wherefore your boasts?

Alas! for the gold of generous sentiments; alas! for the broad humanity that is tender to the core. Three help-

H

less women alone in London, to struggle for existence !
They are fore-doomed, though the process of defeat be a
longer or shorter lengthening out of mortal agony.

Lodgers were to be had in plenty, but, for the most
part, these were as straitened as themselves. Mrs. Amor
had a succession of defaulters, who could not, or would not,
pay the weekly pittance which to her was becoming more
and more important.

Lizzie had obtained teaching in the house of a Mrs.
Black, but only for a few hours daily ; and the remunera-
tion, small to begin with, is made smaller by the omnibus
fare which the distance from her home renders necessary.

Ruth was wholly unsuccessful in her quest for similar
employment. After two months of fruitless endeavour,
and that hope deferred which maketh the heart sick, she
applied for a resident situation in a school and became
teacher there, seeing her mother only at rare intervals.

Lizzie had no love of teaching ; and when a year had
passed in the toil she felt uncongenial, Mrs. Black's sudden intimation that a governess would no longer be required
gave her joy rather than pain.

The young Blacks were to go to school : where Lizzie
was to go was naturally a question of profound indifference
to Mrs. Black. It so happened, however, that on several
occasions the schoolroom had been entered by a friend of
hers, Miss G——, whose brother Jim was a rising star in
the sphere of art ; and the fair complexion, the colour of
hair, the shapely form of the young governess had struck
the eye of the visitor as points of possible value to an
artist.

" It is not the features exactly, Jim," said Miss G——,
" but the colouring, the slope of the shoulders, the pose of
he head, these are lovely ; and she won't cost you much

Mrs. Black had her cheap, I know, and the girl has no other engagement."

" You women would sell your souls for a bargain," cried Jim, in disgust ; "Mrs. Black was always a skinflint. I don't under-pay my models; offer the girl a decent sum ; let us say so much ——"

He was contemplating the personal points his sister had called up to his imagination, and satisfaction of the æsthetic sense invariably kindled tenderness in Jim's bosom.

When, in due form, his offer was laid before Lizzie, she eagerly accepted it ; and hurried home to tell her mother, anticipating, poor child, that she, like herself, would over-flow with gratitude towards their as yet unseen benefactor.

It was not so, however.

Mrs. Amor saw lions in the path, and could not rejoice. Had not Lizzie already pledged her word, she would have refused to sanction this new engagement.

To Lizzie, the reason of this was a pure enigma. She could not fathom her mother's feeling, and since no explanation was vouchsafed, she felt aggrieved. She said nothing of engagements by other artists to which the first led up. Thus mystery was followed by reticence, an evil weed that sprung up in the garden of their love, and in a few short months destroyed the spontaneous happiness of their tender mutual relation.

Lizzie's face grew brighter than before ; the money she earned was gladly poured into Mrs. Amor's lap, but the thoughts and emotions of the girl became as a closed book to her mother, and even the incidents of the art-studio were never disclosed. Mrs. Amor hated the gold that was robbing her of the beloved child whose frankness formerly had equalled her affection.

One day the hour of return from her occupation passed, and no Lizzie appeared! Anxiety grew to agony, and still no relief. Mrs. Amor felt stunned. Then followed two days of frantic efforts, agonized suspense, growing despair, emotions that shook the widow's tottering health to its foundations.

At last came a letter, without date, the post-mark Killarney.

"Dearest mother, don't be unhappy about me; I am married.

"It has grieved me sadly not to tell you all, but my husband knows best, and he says we can't do otherwise just now.

"Darling mother, have Ruth home to be with you at once. I will send all the money I can; and my husband is awfully good.

"We are travelling, so I can't give an address.

"Your loving Lizzie.

"P.S.— I am very, very happy. Love to Ruth."

Mrs. Amor never recovered the blow.

She had a sharp illness, from which she passed into a condition of chronic invalidism, and so remained during the last two years of her life.

Ruth resigned her situation, to tend her mother. On her young shoulders there fell a burden of anxiety and care that seemed to wither up her youth.

The pecuniary help that came from Lizzie dwindled in amount, and then died away; and as no further disclosure was made of her history, Ruth gradually learned to avoid the mention of a name that never failed to upset the dear invalid's nerves and entail fresh suffering upon both.

Relentless poverty now had them in its grasp. For the second time they broke up the home, and sold off their furniture.

Behold them, in lodgings of meagre description, and Ruth is urgently seeking, painfully failing to obtain, employment of almost any kind.

Society—to its shame be it spoken—has no niche for the honourable wage-earner who must devote a portion of daily time to the paramount duty of nursing a dying mother! No, it has none!

Give us all or nothing, is the answer it flings to its humble supplicant for work, and even the Society for Promoting the Employment of Women—that champion of female rights, so nobly ambitious in its projects and promise, so utterly futile in its performance—had no office, and no surety of daily bread for the hapless Ruth.

A little plain sewing, poorly paid, was what its rich lady patrons condescendingly bestowed, and there are long periods of every year, as my reader must surely know, when the rich are out of town, and the poor, who hang upon their skirts, are quietly ignored.

Ruth turned her footsteps slowly one day from the threshold of a handsome West End mansion. A pretty girl there, as young as herself, had said, gaily, to her, " No, Miss Amor, I am thankful to say we start for the Continent to-morrow. I am tired to death of balls, and At Homes, and Matinées. We go straight to Switzerland to recruit. I want no more sewing done at present, thank you. But the bodices you made me are beautifully sewed, and mother said I had paid you too little; so here is two-and-sixpence. That is sixpence more for each, you know."

To Ruth, the proffered half-crown seemed to mock her misery. She had an impulse to reject it, to fling it in the girl's face, so mastering was, for the moment, her anti-social feeling.

Her wretchedness of life was slowly corroding the sweetness of her native disposition, and anger, hatred—nauseous
emotions—would surge in her bosom at every fresh disappointment.

The thought of her mother checked the savage impulse.
She took the coin with a movement of the lips: she meant
to convey a smile.

In the eyes of the giver it seemed a scowl, and drew
forth the remark to her mother—

" What an unpleasant person that Miss Amor is. At
the Society they called her a lady, but I think she is down-
right rude."

With slow steps, and a fainting heart, poor Ruth wended
her way eastwards, pondering the relative importance of
her sick mother's many requirements. It was but little
the half-crown could buy, and of the much that was
wanted, what pressed the most on the invalid was a serious
problem to solve.

Another thought came. Should she take a decisive
step to-day; and, instead of losing hours in hunting for
sewing, offer her services in a milliner's wareroom, and be
absent from her dear one's side from morning till night ?

She paused at a milliner's window ; and in a state of
gathering emotions, argued the point in her mind. The
alternatives were awful to her. She saw them both
clearly : to watch the slow process of starvation, or, to
return each evening in trembling fear, and on some fatal
day, find her darling, beloved mother, no more.

The girl clasped her hands, and threw up her eyes to
heaven in an agony of hesitation, quite unaware of the
fact that a stranger stood at her side, lost in admiration
of the beauty and depth of expression in the sad young
face.

The expression in his face—for the stranger was a young man—betokened surprise, then decision.

He abruptly touched Ruth. She turned upon him her eyes, whose far-away gaze quickly changed into one of child-like and frightened bewilderment.

"I beg your pardon," said the stranger, as he took off his hat and assumed a respectful attitude, going straight to the point, " I am an artist, engaged on a great work. Your face is precisely what I am in search of to complete it. If you will sit to me I shall feel eternally obliged. Money may be no object to you "—he was quite aware of the poverty of her dress, but politeness to so pretty a girl demanded this insincere form of homage,—" but, for my own sake, you will permit me to pay for the service, although, to tell truth, no amount of money would be any real return for the favour I ask."

A quiver passed over Ruth's frame. She cast down her eyes, and put out her hand to the window-frame for support. Then, recovering self-possession, she glanced at the stranger and said, softly, " Oh ! sir ! I do want money. I want it badly. My mother is dying. We are very poor. I will do what you wish, if only," and she gasped with fear lest the stipulation she had hitherto found so obstructive should again prove insurmountable; " you will let me come to you when I can. Not all day long, I dare not leave my mother all day long. But would not four hours each day do for you ? Oh, sir ! for the love of God," and the eyes grew more lovely still in their earnest pleading, " say yes."

" Of course, I say yes," he answered brightly. " You may come to me just when and how you will, within certain limitations, you know. I don't work after six, not even when old king Sol permits !"

Having said this, with a smile, and his hands fumbling in a pocket, he suddenly drew forth, and proffered to her, a sovereign, adding blandly, "A further favour I must ask. That you take this small sum in advance," and, when Ruth shrank back with—"Oh! no! no! It would not be right. I have not earned it."

"Yes, yes," he urged impatiently, "it is right, indeed. But, ah! I forgot, you were never an artist's model before."

At that word Ruth started, and he, taking advantage of her momentary confusion to press the money into her hand, said, "It is customary in my profession. But now I must go. Shall we say, then, to-morrow? What hours will suit you? Not early I suppose. Will two o'clock do? From two till six? I see it will. Thanks."

Ruth had looked her assent, with eyes full of tears.

"Here," he continued, "is my address."

He handed her a card, and, politely lifting his hat, said, "Till to-morrow," and left her.

"James Garrard," was on the card, "No. 3, Fitzroy Street."

Ruth read, and hurried homewards, with a step that, at first, was elastic, joyous, but gradually slowed. A sombre mood again oppressed her, and a difficult question pressed for decision. Dared she tell her mother that she, like Lizzie, had become a model? Could she speak that word to her mother at all?

No! she could not; she must not. It might cost her her life. But, should she then deceive her? Should she pretend the work she had found was daily teaching? Ruth had a keen intellect, she was far more clever than her sister, and instantly there arose to her imagination the distasteful task of parrying a long succession of innocent motherly questions, and a hideous, ever deepening ditch of vile hypocrisy into which she was about to plunge.

Her brain swam, her heart sickened, she tottered, and would have fallen, but a railing was close by. That she grasped, then remembering that her breakfast, hastily swallowed five hours before, had been of the most meagre description, she crept slowly to a confectioner's, and asked for a roll and a glass of milk.

When she left the shop, her resolve was taken. She made purchases, then steadily pursued her way home, but the brain kept repeating over and over in a mechanical way—

"Mother, forgive me. It is only love that makes me false to you. It is only love that makes me false to you."

The hours spent in Mr. Garrard's studio became the one bright spot in Ruth's daily life. Since leaving Ambleside, nowhere, absent from her mother, but in that studio had she encountered the warmth and shelter of human sympathy. In itself it was an abode of comfort and beauty, and Ruth, who took delight in the beautiful, grew to feel quite at home in it.

Every picture there, except one, turned face to the wall, which the artist never showed her, she learned by heart, and felt the richer for.

By her mother's side, in the gloom of their dreary, ugly, almost squalid lodging, her eyes would inwardly feast on some rich landscape, or tranquil scene of happy life, and, with glowing cheeks, she would turn to her mother, kiss her fondly, and babble of the sweetness and joy that would come to them some time.—"Yes, darling, some time, in the world that is to be for meek and lowly ones like you and me."

Mr. Garrard made no encroachments on Ruth's liberty. He welcomed her approach, but never sought to detain her when she chose to return to her mother.

My reader must better understand this character. The man was no generous-minded philanthropist. He was a selfish egotist; good natured in the main, when not thwarted in his purposes, and distinguished by that surface politeness which a society, itself hollow and artificial, accepts in lieu of good manners—the outcome of true, pure, elevated morals.

James Garrard was warm of temperament—that is, he was ardent in devotion to art; ardent also in susceptibility to the attractions of the opposite sex, and in gratification of what *he* called the tender passion.

In this gratification, however, he was capable, at times, of reverting from the semi-civilised creature he was, to a lower type of barbarous man; and compassing his ends by despicable cunning, nay, even by unscrupulous force.

Whilst he was thus primitive in nature, poor Ruth, alas! was primitive in her judgments of mankind.

To her, James Garrard was a hero of romance; a very model of goodness! She to him was simply, at first, his indispensable art-model. By and bye the position changed. Her beauty of feature, her docility, her artless simplicity and frankness, formed a rare combination of attractions to which the artist succumbed. On his side a violent passion sprung up, controlled from day to day by the fear of alarming or offending her. On her side, the feeling that grew, till it seemed to absorb her, body and soul, was a sentiment of mingled worship and generous self-sacrificing love.

She was no longer torn by anxieties concerning her mother's daily bread. The invalid's wants were liberally supplied, and every fresh comfort or luxury that Ruth was enabled to carry to the one beloved bound her by a tender link of grateful love to the other.

It may seem strange to my reader, nevertheless it is a fact, that after weeks of intimacy, Mr. Garrard did not know Ruth's surname, and had not even guessed of the existence of a sister whose loss was the central trial of her life.

He was without curiosity in regard to his fellow-creatures, provided the ego and its interests were not distinctly involved. He loved Ruth ardently, indeed desperately, for had he not resolved he would stop at nothing to win her? He would marry, if that were necessary. By Jove! she was a girl no man need be ashamed to marry; but, to draw from her the details of her personal history, he never thought of it!

True, he questioned her on her mother's state, or sufferings; for, if he wished a touching expression on the sweet face—and she was his Mariana in the moated Grange, and his Blessed Damozel,—he must play upon the vibrating strings of filial love to pitch the delicate instrument in his hands to the required tone.

When the necessity for sadness under his pencil had momentarily passed, he delighted to enthral her by some brisk tale of his own boyish exploits, or lively picture of life in the many sunny lands he had visited, till smiles came back to the tender lips, and the face responded beamingly to the happy thrill of his own vigorous nerves.

She had been prepared from the first to keep her own counsel in reference to Lizzie, but he never dreamed she had a secret to keep; and when it dawned upon her that no duplicity would be required in the studio, her mind was immensely relieved. and she surrounded this trait of

his—a callous indifference to human history, when not
under his eye,—with a halo projected from her own
generous sentiments.   She believed it a masculine virtue
to be sympathetic without asking disagreeable questions!

He had asked her name on the day of her first
appearance in his studio, and she, standing before him
with childlike grace, flushed cheeks, and in a state of
trembling agitation, said, "Ruth," and hesitated.

His fancy took flight at the word.   Ruth! he thought,
Ruth!   How lovely she'd look amid ripe grain in the
strong light of an eastern sky!   Shall I paint her so, and
not immediately as Mariana?

Whether she told him her surname or not he never
knew, and later he did not care to ask.   Henceforth she
was his Ruth; "the one Ruth," he would say to himself,
"he had ever known, and the one woman whom he had
ever truly loved."

Love's young dream now encompassed Ruth Amor.   She
lived an ideal life, although wholly in the present.

Tender words and caresses had been bestowed by the
artist; and she felt, though she could not have borne the
expression of the thought, that when otherwise homeless,
his love would be naturally her shelter and home.

"Mine wholly, some day, my darling," was whispered
in her ear; and to her warm, yet shrinking response: "But
not soon; oh! pray God with me, not soon," came:

"Well, see Ruth, how good and patient I am, kiss me
my love."   And Ruth hastened from him, to pour out her
tenderness without stint on her mother, and rekindle the
smouldering embers of life by the radiance of her own inward happiness.

A month had passed thus when one day Ruth was conscious of a change in the atmosphere of the studio.   The

artist was silent, distrait; moreover, he looked ill, as though he had not slept. Ruth asked no questions, but her heart palpitated with affectionate sympathy.

Suddenly a footstep was heard on the threshold and the door-handle was turned from outside. No entrance, however, followed. The door had been locked within.

A violent rapping began. Mr. Garrard flung down his brush, crossed the room with hasty step, passed outside, closing the door behind him; and engaged in an angry altercation with someone who stood there. To Ruth's intense surprise, the tones mingling with his were those of a woman!

An impulse of delicacy made her thrust her fingers into her ears, but, in spite of the precaution, a phrase, shrilly uttered, struck upon the tympanum with all the force of a mortal blow.

"I am your wife, James Garrard! I am your wife!"

Ruth fell back in her chair, and lost consciousness.

When recalled to herself *he* was with her, in gentle accents imploring her to say what had alarmed his darling. "Look up, Ruth, my love, I am here! Did you think I had left you?"

She drew herself back, stumbled to her feet, and looking at him with the gaze of a stricken deer, moaned softly: "I did not know you were married, indeed I did not. No wonder your wife has been angry. I will, go."

"Go!" he cried impetuously; "you? Ruth! you go? Good God! are women all mad together!" Then, with a sudden change to accents of overwhelming tenderness and pathos—"*You* are my wife, Ruth! I have no one to love me but *you,* and now you are cruel—"O, Ruth!" reproachfully, "do you wish to leave me, to forsake me, because I am in trouble? My love should be generous. Ruth! I implore you! come to me now. Give yourself wholly. I love you, I love you, my dearest! Come, live with me," and tears of self pity welling into his eyes, he stretched forth his arms.

She flung herself into their embrace, and clung to him.

A great wave of sympathetic emotion swept over the girl's soul, followed by a paroxysm of tender passion. Ruth was dead for the hour to every impression save one—her beloved was unhappy; she must love him, console him, do all he desired; if need be, die for him.

The work of the studio was never resumed that day. An hour later Ruth emerged from the house agitated, but with an expression of resolve in her face. She turned homewards, and had reached the corner of the street, when again she was startled. A hand roughly placed on her shoulder, made her wheel round abruptly. Behold! she stood face to face with her sister Lizzie, the sister whom she had not seen for two years!

In joyful surprise she cried out: "Oh, Lizzie!" and stopped appalled. The face before her was distorted by hideous passions—hatred, horror, revenge, looked forth from the eyes, and the white lips slowly opened, to hiss out, "It was *you* who robbed me of my husband's heart; *you*, Ruth, my sister!" A spasm of mortal agony seized her. The voice became hoarser still. "O God! he deceived me— he gave me only a false name." Then, with eyes fixed on Ruth, who stood motionless, she seemed striving to recall the past, when a footstep was heard behind; she turned and precipitately fled.

The stranger who approached, found Ruth white as a sheet.

"Are you ill, young lady?" he asked, and caught her, as she fell fainting, in his arms.

To a chemist's close by he carried her, and waited her recovery impatiently. He was a business man, a stock-broker, who might be loser of thousands of pounds by delay of a few moments. Alas! when the dictates of common humanity traverse the interests of the pocket!

Ruth at last looked round bewildered, and rose to her feet, asking anxiously what had happened? where was she? what was the hour? Her protector hailed gladly this half-recovery; assured her she was all right; called a cab, placed her in it, and, giving from her lips to the driver the address of Mrs. Amor's lodging, hurried off relieved.

O, Ruth! child of misfortune, like the many thousands whose agonies we shall never know; was it some mitigation of thy cruel fate that the poor brain was already stunned into numbness, when there fell on thee the last fearful blow of that fateful day?

She crept feebly upstairs, and entered the room where lay a still form. She approached the bed, and what, at another time, would have filled her heart to bursting, caused no explosion now.

Death—its calmness, its stillness was everywhere, within her, around her.

She touched the cold hand, the marble brow; she gazed at the half-open eyes, the lips that seemed to breathe upon her an ineffable repose; and, confusedly throwing off her hat and cloak, she stretched herself on the bed, and gathered into her embrace the motionless form of her dead mother, whispering to herself again and again—"I, too, am dead."

Hours passed away. How many, I cannot say. When at last the landlady appeared on the threshold, Ruth was asleep, with her dead in her arms.

Aroused suddenly, somewhat harshly, the delicate brain of the bereaved girl was unable to bear the shock of agony. She gave way to a wild phrensy, and when thrust aside in the household bustle that followed upon discovery of Mrs. Amor's death, poor Ruth fled aimlessly from the house, and returned to it no more.

Mrs. Amor's burial was a desolate one. No loved one was near. The expenses were paid by a gentleman, whose unexpected appearance on the scene formed an important part, in the landlady's view, of the tragedy that had occurred in her house.

"He came the second day after Miss Amor was lost," she was wont to relate, "asking eagerly for a sick lady, whose daughter bore the christian name of Ruth, and when I told him both was gone, and Miss Amor had left all her clothes—which my husband thought was only right, for there seemed no money about them to pay the funeral, and Mrs. Amor was always one as liked things nice."

"'Amor!' says he, 'Amor! did you say?' quite sharp like; and down he sits, as though he had been took with a spasm.

"He questioned me after that, and so as I never was questioned before about lodgers. Thinks I to myself, what these ladies is to you, and you to them, it beats me to tell; but he were as real a gentleman, and as handsome as ever I saw. He wrote a letter to Miss Amor, and left it with me, and he came every day for a week, and just a few times after that."

It was not on the second, but the third day from Mrs. Amor's death, that a girl, half drowned, was rescued from the river Thames, and conveyed to the parish poor-house.

From there a message was sent to Islington, which brought quickly to the bedside of the unhappy Ruth Mrs.

M. Williams, one of those devoted women whose christianity prompts to noble deeds of tender humanity.

What her wanderings in the interval had been, Ruth never knew. When the delirium of brain fever had passed, and in prostration of strength she lay waiting the daily visitor, whose kind face and gentle voice reading the Bible was the only pleasant break in the weary, monotonous hours, she would try in dumb agony to recall the events of her history up to the end of that fatal day. Her meeting with Lizzie she remembered, alas! alas!—and even dimly did she see her mother's calm features and rigid form, but there memory stopped.

The brain had no record further till the new history began of impressions within these four walls—weakness, sadness, pain, and no relief save what lay in Mrs. Williams' soothing prayers and gentle womanly words.

Earnest petitions were raised to Almighty God that a hard heart might be broken; that Ruth might turn from evil ways, and enter on a holier life. Petitions that to the stricken girl conveyed little meaning, whilst the soft touch, the sweet smile, the sympathetic kiss that followed the prayers were of healing efficacy; and in time Ruth sobbed forth in the arms of her new friend all of her history that she was able to tell.

When convalescence was advanced, Mrs. Williams took Ruth to her home in Islington, and rejoicing that her beautiful hair had been cut, put a cap on her head, gave her the name of Mary Jones, and installed her there as domestic servant.

The position proved embarrassing to the good lady. She feared Mr. Garrard might discover his victim, in spite of disguise; and the idle curiosity of neighbours was an annoyance.

Ruth's beauty, her extreme gravity, her comparative ignorance of domestic work, drew observation upon her. She was one of Mrs. Williams' protégées, and clearly must have a history. Hence questions were asked, which to reply to would neither be kind nor discreet. Mrs. Williams became increasingly anxious for Ruth's present safety, for the virtuous peace of her future.

She herself was aged, childless, and victim to a morbid action of the heart that might at any time suddenly end her life; and what of Ruth then?

She must emigrate, thought Mrs. Williams; there is no help for it. She must leave London for Australia, the colonies, anywhere abroad, so soon as I make her proficient in domestic work.

Tenderly did she broach the subject to poor Ruth; but the effect was paralysing.

The creature ordinarily so docile, quiescent, still, quivered in every nerve, and with tearless sobbing, clung to her friend, crying piteously: "*Must* I go? oh! say, *must* I go? I have no one to love me, no one I love but you! O, God, let me die; I do so wish to die!"

The question was dropped. It remained in abeyance, and a month passed away. Then there happened an unexpected, and to Mr. and Mrs. Williams, a welcome event. The former is an intelligent man, observant of every social movement indicative of industrial or moral progress. Into his hands there fell at this juncture a journal called the "Commonweal," where he read an article written by Henri Martin. His theme was the well-worn one—England's hideous contrasts of wealth and poverty—the heart-rending position of thousands unable by honest work to earn subsistence in a country overflowing with wealth. Socialism the only remedy—an entire new system of industry, in which competition, private property in land and in capital, have no place.

For the securing of that fundamental remedy, said the writer, the times are as yet unripe. Meanwhile special and minor reformative action in right directions should be urged and aided. Then followed a full description of the Unitary Home at Peterloo; an account of the principles and aims of the founders; and finally an invitation to all readers interested in this experiment to view it for themselves at certain given hours, and critically judge of the same.

Eagerly did Mr. and Mrs. Williams avail themselves of this invitation. They travelled to Peterloo, and had many interviews with Miss José, Margaret, and others of our Unitary Home. They placed the whole facts of Ruth's history before the General Council, and the result was, that after some weeks the desolate girl was under the roof of La Maison.

In the happier days that slowly but surely dawned for the gentle Ruth, she was seated one morning in the old house at Islington, whither she had gone to visit her friends, by Mrs. Williams' side. Looking frankly in her face, she said softly, " Yes, indeed I am happy, so happy there. I love them all. So would you, though they are not Christians."

"Not Christians? Ah, well, my dear!" the old lady replied, "there are too many sects in the present day; but it is the Lord's work your friends are doing; for, has He not said in His own blessed word—and reverently she touched the Bible lying near to her,—' He setteth the solitary in families.'"

I—2

CHAPTER IX.

VERA'S HOPES AND GRIEFS.

WHEN two young people of the upper middle-class marry, and set up an establishment in the ordinary way, the husband, who has exchanged a bachelor life, and it may be a very solitary lodging, for a home, finds his day-dreams fulfilled—for at least the first few months.

To the wife there are drawbacks. She has made a gain and a loss.

Her old home, possibly, nay probably, was brimful of family life, and bright with the sunshine of family love. Now, she has hours of dreary solitude, and many domestic responsibilities and perplexities new to her.

The first year of married life is an epoch of varied experience, very trying, often dangerous to feminine nerves. The emotional state predominates; fluctuations from rapturous joy to moods of depression occur, and in view of the conjugal union, that has yet to be deepened, consolidated, this unstable equilibrium of the young wife is, to say the least, jeopardous.

The whole position, however, in the case of Vera and Joe Ferrier was reversed. Joe's day-dreams had not been fulfilled, nor even approached. Was that the fault of the dreams or of the reality? the phantasm or the substance? My reader must judge for himself.

116

Like most fine young men of the present day, he had had admirers of the opposite sex.

Some of these were more showy, and some more gifted than Vera; but the fact that they made advances to him, whilst she made none, had a striking effect on Joe's haughty, combative, even perverse, disposition. He selected his wife under promptings of a mingled nature. He singled out the simple, retiring Vera, and with conscious generosity bestowed his affection on her.

The joy she evinced was doubly becoming—it showed her not only responsive to his affection, but slightly subdued by the honour he did her; and this riveted the links between them.

Vera, grateful for his young love, was, in Joe's eyes, an attractive picture, and, as in his day-dreams the future took shape, Vera, his wife, continued adorned with that graceful mantle of gratitude.

In the home, where he had hoped to instal her, the little woman would be all his own. She will part with him pensive each morning, and hail him at night with effusive emotion; the sunshine of love and of life will reach her only through him; and every addition to their household gods, hardly earned by his labour, will make her more grateful, more loving than before.

Now, the facts of their married life had been different. For one short week they were away together, but only in the solitude of crowded London, in places of public amusement, hotels, and railway carriages. To his dismay, too, he had perceived that Vera, with naïve simplicity, would readily have foregone even this short week in order to assist Margaret in preparing La Maison for its inmates, and removing her mother from the old home to the new.

During the wedding tour, Vera's state of mind was one

of divided interests, and no sooner were they settled in
the Commune than an extraordinary animation possessed
her.   The timid, emotional, lady-like Vera became transformed into an active, bustling little wife, whom her
husband seemed hardly to know!   He put no question to
himself concerning this change : but there are mysterious
parts of the human brain that act independently of conscious will; and for the first two months Joe's mind was
full of alarmed sensitiveness lest the popularity of his wife
should interfere with the marital rights of his somewhat
exacting affection.

But Vera rose to the occasion.   Her nature is strong
and expansive on the emotional side.   If the claims upon
her are many, many also are her powers of responsive
affection ; and it is precisely because these powers were
not required in the old home that there she had often been
miserable ; whilst here, with her best faculties called into
play, she was happy as a bird.

Her duties in the morning were manifold ; but whilst
Joe, on awaking, had languor, inertia to overcome, she
would spring from his side, cheer him with lively talk,
and when dressed in the calico, or homespun, in which he
was bound to confess his darling looked the lady still, she
parted from him lovingly, to greet with affection the
workers upstairs, and accomplish the service apportioned
to her, whether in the kitchen, refectory, or elsewhere.
When breakfast was over, a few moments could generally
be spared for young wives to be with their husbands.

Frank Ray had retained his occupation in Liverpool,
as well as Joe Ferrier.   On fine mornings Vera would put
on her hat to accompany Joe, with cigar in his mouth,
round the garden, and say farewell at the gate as he
started for town.   Again in the evenings they could be

alone if they wished. In the salon there is always a bright
little party assembled. There Mrs. Ward has her whist-
table, and often her old friend, Mr. Scott, as partner. But
the young, as is natural, flit from one to another of the
various public rooms. The music and conversation rooms
are usually occupied, and the play-room, till nine o'clock,
contains, as a rule, a merry group.

Joe's tendency to isolation, an isolation that comprised
—would absorb if it dared—his wife, was perceptible from
the first.

When coffee was over, and Vera not required, as occasionally she was in the kitchen for half an hour, Joe would
call her away to a parlour, or the billiard-room, and secure
for himself an hour or two of strictly domestic, marital
privacy and felicity. To smoke with only Vera beside him
was at least an approach to his original day-dream! He
never forgot the lesson Mr. Spiers had given him on the
true relations of the sexes.

He often remarked : " I've thrown in my lot with these
reformers, who go in for women's rights and that sort of
thing—I am bound to conform ;" and indeed his inherited
gentlemanly instincts rendered his behaviour towards the
general group in all essentials irreproachable. Nevertheless, as is common in the process of evolution, an old form
tends to persist in some trifling particular, and Joe, with
his changed ideas, would at times address Vera in a tone
of possessive authority that betokened an unfit survival!

Now, one of the characteristics of an expanded domestic
life is its facilities for comparison. It affords a new field
for conscious natural selection. Here all the delicate relations of human life with the inherited manners and
customs that cling about these relations will be closely
observed, and put to the test, and only such will survive

as broadly merit survival by ministering to man's social wants in promoting his sweetness, goodness, and happiness.

To Vera, Joe, before marriage appeared simply perfect. One month of the Commune revealed some defects!

On her ear, Frank Ray's tone to his wife struck differently from Joe's to herself. No wonder this was so!

Frank sprang from the people, and Joe from a class whose dominancy had endured for upwards of a thousand years! Vera, however, was no philosopher, and to her, had she known it, this explanation would not have made less disagreeable the disagreeable fact.

To her credit be it told that three months of their life in La Maison were completed before the inward jar proclaimed itself in an ebullition of temper; and moreover, there was in Vera's condition a physical cause for nerve-disturbance of which she was only dimly conscious, and Joe not conscious at all.

The two were lingering on the staircase one evening on their way to the billiard-room, when Percy Cairns ran out from the play-room, and breathlessly assailed Vera, flinging his arms round her skirts—he could not reach to her waist,—and looking up in her face, " Dear Vera, we are going to act charades! Come, help us! Do, do! Ruth is coming, and Lucy, and Rose—and—and——." Before she could answer, Joe promptly repulsed the child. " Have done, sir," he said. " Are these your manners to a lady? Let go her dress; Vera is going to play billiards with me."

A tempest of anger sprang up in poor Vera, and shook her from all self-control.

She stooped and embraced the boy, saying audibly: "Never mind what he says. I will come to the play-room in half-an hour." Then, with flushed cheeks, and a defiant air, she turned to accompany Joe.

He entered a parlour, and closed the door. "Do you think, Vera," he said, calmly facing the excited girl with a slightly magisterial air, "do you think your behaviour just now was that of a good and effectionate wife? There's a confounded lot of nonsense talked here about example to children, but your example, if you teach them that wives are not bound to consider their husbands' wishes ——"

He suddenly paused, for Vera had burst into tears!

During the last few weeks her mind had dwelt speculatively upon a possible future, and the mental condition created all manner of emotional changes—hope, joy, timidity, absolute fear, and withal a background of delicious tenderness. The moment was critical, and no words her husband could utter would have stung her so sharply as this allusion to children, and her personal influence on them! Poor Vera! But the tears did not soften: angry words poured hotly from her lips—"If I am not fit to be with children, neither are you. You don't love them—I see that. Oh! why did I marry, till I knew ——"

It was Joe's turn now to be stung to the quick. His masterful mood had vanished at sight of her tears, and he had eagerly approached Vera, intending to gently caress and console; but, behold him fiercely maligned! and for what? "Confound it," he thought; "does she really expect me to love all these brats?" The unreasonableness of this surmised folly exasperated him. "Come, Vera!" he remonstrated in a high-pitched key, "This is too absurd!"

Again he pulled up, for the torrent pent in his wife's bosom broke forth. "That is always the way with you, Joe," she cried; "you pooh-pooh my feelings—you don't respect me as Frank respects Rose! You command me to do this and that! Why am I to consider your wishes

always, and you not consider mine ?   I don't want to play
billiards; it tires me."

"Oh! well," Joe interrupted, with a haughty gesture,
"you are quite at liberty, Vera, to spend your evenings as
you like best; it will be long before I ask you again to
spend one with me ; " and, turning on his heel, he abruptly
left the room.

Vera flung herself on the sofa, and struggled to suppress
a fit of hysterical sobbing : then she fled upstairs, plunged
her face in cold water, and in a quarter of an hour was
the centre of a hilarious group in the play-room.   It was
she who that night tucked his crib blanket round little
Percy's shoulders, and gave him a motherly hug; and at
ten o'clock she was restlessly moving to and fro in the
nursery, with the baby clasped in her arms and tears
streaming down her cheeks.

Next day a bustling activity characterised Vera.   Her
housemaid duties not being burdensome, she instituted an
unnecessary cleaning in her mother's room.   It was not
till 4 p.m. that Margaret, who had noted the flush on
her cheek all day, persuaded her to rest on a couch in one
of the parlours, and surreptitiously brought in Dr. Basil to
afternoon tea.

As he entered, the young doctor exclaimed, "Why,
Vera! how tired you look; let me feel your pulse! " then
gravely, "I think, my good comrade, you should go to
bed."

The answer was a scornful laugh.

To Margaret, after leaving the room, he said, "Try to
get her to bed; she is ill—very feverish.   H s anything
happened to annoy or distress her ?   I have known for
some time she—I mean her condition is delicate, but this
feverish excitement—I will stay whilst you urge her —"

But Margaret's entreaties were vain. Vera was wilful, perverse, irrational. "I am well enough," she said angrily. "Don't tease me, Margaret; and pray! don't put any nonsense into Joe's head."

Her friends were compelled to desist.

After dinner, at which poor Vera ate nothing, she said coldly to Joe, "I wish to play billiards this evening. I suppose you don't care to play with me—I'll ask Walter Cairns."

"Do just as you like," her husband replied, with freezing politeness.

An hour later the billiard-room was occupied. The doctor was there, and Margaret, with Walter and Vera; and Joe hovered round them, keenly watching the game. Vera played better than usual. She had just achieved a brilliant stroke, when Lucy, coming close to her elbow (Vera, engrossed with the play, had not seen her enter), whispered, "Your mother has had a bad fall! Can you come to her quickly?"

Vera turned round to Lucy with a blanched cheek and vacant gaze. The next instant she lay on the ground, whilst Joe, who had run to her, frantically strove to restore animation, and Dr. Basil promptly opened the window.

Mrs. Ward's fall was a trifling occurrence, but Vera's was the precursor of a serious illness. Joe Ferrier's pride had its fall! His self-confident nature was profoundly shaken when the doctor enlightened him on the subject of Vera's maternal hopes, now, alas! destroyed; and added, "Some nerve disturbance, the source of which I am unable to trace, had altered the conditions and made imminent this catastrophe, which Lucy's news, too abruptly given, only precipitated."

The sick nursing that young Mrs. Ferrier received was

a true ministration of love.   She was dearly beloved by the
whole household, and so far from her tendance being felt
as a task, it was regarded by all the sisterhood, and some
of the brotherhood, as a privilege.

In domestic life of the old regime, the trained nurse
is a new institution of questionable merit!   When
sickness occurs in a household of—say, the upper
middle class, a perfect stranger takes possession of the
sick-room, and banishes all the dear, familiar faces from
the patient's longing eyes.   There are cases, no doubt,
in which this is necessary, to avoid the spread of disease;
but in thousands of cases it is merely done as a matter of
custom, and what it brings about is pain to devoted
friends, and to the patient no gain, but a loss in comfort,
for skill without love—though it may be an improvement
on love without skill—is only a makeshift, a partial one-
sided supply of the real, the all-round requirements.

In associated domestic life alone will the final development take place; and martyrs to physical suffering will
there be relieved from all pain, not inevitable, by surroundings in which skill and love are well interwoven and
closely combined.

La Maison, however, is only as yet inaugurating the
new system, and nothing within it is perfect.   Illness had,
of course, been foreseen, and prepared for to some extent
by anticipation.   No disorganisation of the household it
was resolved must occur, and no overwork to any special
member.   Labour from without must be brought in on
emergency, but only to assist in kitchen, housework, etc.,
and not to perform any of the higher domestic functions.

Mrs. Plimsoll, Margaret, and Mr. Spiers, had each some
experience in sick nursing, and, with a doctor at hand
to direct and guide them, their skill was certain to im-

prove. The younger members would assist in rotation, and, so far as the state of the patient permitted, be properly trained in the art.

Vera was efficiently nursed, and Joe, in his mood of tender, half self-reproachful regret, flung his notions of sex distinctions in work to the wind, and aided in the task. He said graciously to Margaret, one morning, when anxiety still prevailed, " I am thankful I leave her in your hands! After all, at such times, a commune, no doubt, is better than love in a cottage." And Margaret knew this meant much from poor Joe, so she gratefully smiled in his face.

When convalescence set in, a change in Joe's feelings took place. He and Vera had had their first quarrel, his marital severity had been too great—he would own that, and would ask her forgiveness; but still, his wife, too, had been wrong. She was bound to honour her husband; indeed, the Church says obey! He would waive the obedience—some women are touchy on that point; but Vera had clearly dishonoured him that night, and before the child! " I will talk to her," he said to himself, and the sentiment underneath this expression was: I will gently and kindly rebuke her!

To this end he began one evening as he sat by her couch, assuming a tone of delicate banter, " The burnt child dreads the fire, my love, and you and I will dread quarrels, I fancy, after this wretched disaster! I mean to be an awfully good husband! Will you——"

Vera suddenly withdrew her hand from his grasp, and clasping the other, pressed both on her forehead. Then began a tearless sobbing, amidst which words came brokenly. " Oh! Joe! Joe! why did we marry? —You don't understand me the least, and I!—I love you, I *do* love you—but my love is not perfect—I see all your faults. When the child, *our* child was with me, at times I seemed almost to hate." Sobs choked her a little, but again she resumed, "I saw you so cold, so harsh to children! I thought, an innocent life is here, and no nest of real love prepared in the father's bosom. Oh, Joe! it cannot be right to bring a child into the world if one of the parents does not desire it—long for it as a precious treasure—and what—if it were not happy? We are not fit to be parents—you and I! Indeed we are not fit! I am glad, not sorry, for what has happened."

Here was a turning of the tables. Joe rose to his feet feeling stunned. His little wife—not grateful! but critical! passing judgment on him! A flame of resentment shot up within him, then fluttered and died out. The reflective mood prevailed. Joe slowly faced the position; he recognised the fact that a simple innocent girl may have depths that he could not fathom. For the first time he felt awed, reverent, before the mystery of womanhood.

In another fortnight Vera resumed her household duties, and a new phase of married life began for the young couple. Both were to some extent altered, and Joe had, strange to say, submitted himself voluntarily to authoritative dictation on a matter of purely personal conduct.

In La Maison the power of bringing fresh human life into existence is bound to be controlled in unfavourable conditions by unhurtful scientific methods. No massacre of innocents is permitted there, and the birth of unhealthy infants is pronounced nothing else, *in an epoch of conscious evolution.*

For unhealthy persons to become parents is a crime

against Humanity. Vera for the present is delicate. The responsibilities, the joys of parenthood, must be guarded against, deliberately relinquished till health is fully restored.

It was no longer shrinking timidity, as before marriage, nor bustling activity, as after, that now characterised Vera, but a frank serenity, a gentle dignity betokening growth in the highest of human attributes, viz., sweetness and light. She and Joe spent their evenings together, but seldom alone. The study of physiology was engaged in *au serieux* by both. A class for instruction in this science had been organized under the roof of La Maison, and to it outsiders were made freely welcome. Three evenings in the week the class met, and Joe and Vera attended it regularly.

It was rarely, however, that a whole evening passed without a visit, however short, to the children. "I tell you what, Spiers," Joe had said to his friend; "perhaps a fellow like me should try to develop the paternal instinct." And joyfully Vera noted the fact that, whereas at first the little ones seemed shy of her husband, their confidence rapidly grew, till by-and-bye he had but to show his face in their midst to be hailed with delight, and drawn into their play with such welcome as only children can give.

Before a year had expired, two events occurred of general interest to the whole domesticated group. First, the young doctor was married, and brought his wife home to La Maison; second, his sister Rose Ray gave birth to a daughter. This event created quite a breeze of parental emotions through the household. The young girls were carried away in its sweep, and apathetic bachelors, even, were kindled somewhat to sympathy.

It was Vera who first held that child in her arms, and daintily clothed her to receive a primary benediction from father, grandfather, adoptive brothers, sisters, the whole communal group—a truly wide field of potential relations in which the young life unfolding will not fail to reap a rich harvest of love.

Frank's daughter was prattling small words and totteringly learning to walk when a son was born to Vera, and Joe heard, with unspeakable joy and relief, Dr. Basil's reassuring words, " All is right, my dear fellow; the boy is healthy and sound."   As for Vera, she looked in his face, some four days later, with an expression that brought to his mind their courtship days, and, pressing to her bosom the precious mite of humanity, babbled, as though herself a happy child:

> " Where did you come from, Baby, dear ?
> Out of the everywhere into here.
> Where did you get your eyes so blue?
> Out of the sky as I came through !"
"No ! No ! Joe my darling, he got them from you !"

CHAPTER X.

YOUNG LIFE IN LA MAISON.

Mr. Charles Hunter, a Liverpool merchant, was seated in the breakfast-room of his villa at Peterloo, reading the morning journal, and smoking. "Look, here, Jessie, he called to his wife, who, breakfast being over, was moving about the room : then, taking the cigar from his mouth, he pointed to an advertisement. She began to read it aloud : "In La Maison a school is now open for day boarders or day scholars, from eleven a.m. to one o'clock and from two p.m. to five o'clock." "Here!" he said, "here is the point for us," somewhat impatiently pointing to a paragraph further on. To it his wife passed and again read : "No holidays at stated intervals are given."

"That shows, to my mind," said Mr. Hunter, "that these are sensible people. If there is one piece of folly greater than another in the present foolish system of education, it is the giving of such absurdly long holidays. You know, surely, how Lotta and Blanche never gain anything in the holidays; and, in my opinion, they lose a great deal. It is nonsense to think that children require change of air from a place like this! And for two months, forsooth, each year! No end of expense parents are put to ; and as for comfort— Do you remember, at Scarbro' last summer, how miserable the children were, because no school-companions chanced to be near them? And at Christmas, Lotta lounged about all day reading trashy novels till the skating and parties began together."

"Well! it wasn't *her* fault, Charles, that the frost came the very day of Mrs. Marlow's party!"

"Did I say it was her fault, my dear? I am merely commenting on facts. The child lived in a whirl of excitement for ten days or more, and then broke down. That feverish attack cost us a doctor's bill and the loss of some weeks' schooling."

"But, Charles! these people are peculiar! I heard Mr. Field say so. And they don't go to church! Surely you would not——oh! don't, please, entrust Blanche and Lotta to their care!"

"Field is an idiot! Never quote him to me," cried Mr. Hunter, going off, as he frequently did, on a side issue when answering his illogical wife. "Field is in with that bubble Company again—the new Arizona! Ha-ha! As a director, too! The pious merchants, my dear, are about the greatest speculators I know——."

"Charles! I do wish you would not scoff at religion."

"No, no, Jessie, I do not scoff at all religion. I know *you're* a good woman." Mr. Hunter blandly looked at his wife, and placed one hand on her shoulder. "Let us see," he then said, coaxingly, "what is said about applying at that school;" and taking up the journal: "Ah! the hour to apply is from five to nine. I shall go there this evening."

Without waiting for further remark, he promptly buttoned his coat, and put on an air of business on hand, —not-to-be-trifled-with, as he bade his wife good-bye, and hurried off to town.

At a quarter past five o'clock of the same day he pre-

sented himself at the gate of La Maison. He was conducted to the visitors' room, on the basement floor, where
Walter Cairns received him. The school curriculum was
explained to Mr. Hunter, with the system of education
pursued—no prize-giving, no cramming or straining of a
child's natural powers, no artificial stimulus of any kind ;
no competition in class ; but in all work, co-operation,
self-help and mutual help, with only such emulation as is
free of anti-social feeling.

"You don't mean to turn out stuck-up prigs and strong-
minded females ! that is clear," said Mr. Hunter. "Well,
if my young ones were boys, I can't say your system would
strike me as quite the thing: a man must fight like his
fellows wherever he is ! He must compete and struggle, and
may have to trample down a fellow competitor to make
way for himself in the world's market. Greek and Latin
are no good—I am glad they seem nowhere much with
you ; but competition—a boy is the better for *that*, and for
anything, no matter what, that sharpens his wits. However, I have no boys, as it happens: mine are lasses, as we
Scotchmen say, and I don't want them to take up any of the
eccentricities fashionable amongst their sex ! That higher
education of women is making fools of us all. What with
Girton scholars, platform orators, the shrieking sisterhood,
as *The Saturday Review* well called them, and it might
have added the pottering sisterhood—women, for ever in
back slums, coddling the poor and catching infection,—I
wonder where a sensible man is to look by-and-by for a
wife who will stay quietly at home and attend to the
family ?"

A somewhat sad smile flitted across Walter Cairns'
features as he remarked politely: "You allow nothing for
change in masculine type ? I fancy many men want

κ 2

more from a wife than your picture of haus-frau well covers. The need for equal companionship grows fast in the race ——"

Mr. Hunter hastened to interrupt. *He* wanted no discussion on questionable points, and that word "race" was indicative of dangerous ground. He viewed mankind subjectively from a lofty mercantile eminence, and was quite prepared to be tolerant of some weakness—a mild insanity, even—in these educationists, if only it were not forced upon his notice. "Oh! that," he said, with an air of agreement, "no doubt; but a man gets companionship, plenty, in his club. He wants his wife to be sensible, certainly; and that is what I like in your course"—he looked at Mr. Cairns with expansiveness—a broad expression of patronising approval : "You teach the useful, I observe, rather than the ornamental—not classics, but science. For holidays, you give single days at intervals, as wanted to refresh the pupils, and not in a stretch, to the weariness of parents and considerable loss to the children. My dear sir, that is admirable! Moreover, you take the young ones to skate, or an excursion now and then, and are responsible for them on holidays as well as ordinary days. What a relief to parents! You are on the right track there! Why, my wife and I have never had a pleasant journey or outing alone together since our children were born!" This was said in the tone of a man with a grievance; then suddenly recovering cheerfulness: "But your hour for commencing the daily lessons is a late one: eleven o'clock, did you say?"

"For scholastic work," Mr. Cairns replied—"book learning, acquirements in literature, science, etc., eleven o'clock; but, previous to that there are lessons given all over the house in domestic labour and economic art.

Our children take part in the household work from the earliest possible age; and it belongs to our theory of education—I must ask you to study our formulated principles here "—offering a printed sheet,—"to place the essential duties of life in the foremost position. We spare no pains in the training of young eyes, ears and hands to the intelligent performance of domestic functions. This we regard as a necessary broad foundation for culture, extended knowledge, and general attainments."

"H'm—do you mean," said Mr. Hunter, "you teach cooking before eleven? I should like my girls to learn that. Do you not admit your day scholars to these lessons?"

" We assume that the home is the best place."

"That is nonsense, my dear sir," Mr. Hunter exclaimed; "you are wrong there. The generality of mothers teach their daughters nothing in these days. I don't say they are to blame; girl's won't have it! But look here, Mr. Cairns; raise your fees if you like; I am not the man to grudge the fair payment of labour"—the accent here was pompous; "only take Lotta and Blanche from ten o'clock, and teach them to make themselves generally useful. I'll do what I can to recommend your school." He took up his hat as though the arrangements were now completed. Walter, however, remarked with a grave and dignified air, "There is much for consideration before a final engagement is formed. Our primary object is to promote a worthy ideal of life, not to make money; and I fear," with a smile, " our ideal differs very considerably from yours! Pray bring Mrs. Hunter during school hours, and examine for yourselves the working of our system. If your opinion continues favourable, we shall require the attendance of your daughters for a week previous to the Committee

Meeting, which decides whether they are to be accepted as pupils or not."

Mrs. Hunter received, in fear and trembling, her husband's instructions to visit the school alone. His time was too valuable to expend more on a subject he looked on as comparatively trifling : besides, his mind was made up.—By the way, she must be cautious, circumspect. "These people, my dear, have their own ideas on education. They give no Bible-lessons—they leave that to mothers, and quite right too. They are particular what children they admit; but of course Blanche and Lotta will be gladly received, unless you offend them by some remark. We have really nothing to do with their opinions, Jessie. I am satisfied the education they give is excellent."

Opinions and education stood quite unrelated, in Mr. Hunter's generalization! Anything of the nature of figures, statistics, bears weight, to his mind, and is worthy of close observation; but opinions, if not immediately demonstrable in practical shape, are vague, intangible— of the nature of the " baseless fabric of a vision," though he would not have quoted Shakespeare to explain his views— these certainly need never affect the balance of decision in regard to a school for his daughters.

He gave no further thought to their education that day. How could he ? His energies were required for "business" which he considered of far wider significance. He went upon 'Change for an hour, and his sport there resulted in personal gain—an acquisition of wealth that in its non-relation to production in any form is of no more general utility than plunder; he did honour to a national princeling at a Cake and Wine Banquet; he opened letters in his office, and directed clerks to reply to them; he dropped into his club for luncheon, scanned the journals and gossiped a little on politics and aristocratic scandal; he attended a Bank Meeting and pocketed a handsome fee, although no effort of brain, no mental labour was entailed; he spoke from the platform, at the annual meeting of an Orphan Asylum—spoke, with pathos, of the " miserable struggle for existence going on," and with pompous inflation of " the noble work we are doing amongst orphans; " he handed to the secretary his yearly subscription, precisely one third of the sum he had earned by his valuable presence for one hour at the Bank; and then slipped from the room to enjoy the peace and comfort of his luxurious home with a perfectly easy conscience.

Mr. Hunter believed that he, like the blacksmith of brawny arm, had all that day been administering telling blows, and by "something accomplished, something done," he had " earned his night's repose ! "

Does my reader know the game of whist, and the value of position there ? Is the game of life not similar ? How comes it that some men have only to talk a little, to show themselves here and there, to be outwardly bland, inwardly unscrupulous, and lo! society upholds them, supports them, willingly, gratefully ? They have position, and they know how to pose. Meanwhile the real workers toil on—ah! so wearily! Gifted natures, weighted with precious jewels of truth, are allowed to sink in the social scale, and everywhere rages a conflict that submerges the noblest fruits of Humanity, and brings to the surface the lowest, meanest forms !

Alas! for the wisdom of man! But at least he no longer blasphemes with the impious postulate of an All-wise Divine Creator, impotent to produce a better world; a juster, truer, nobler, happier society than this.

Mrs. Hunter timidly approached La Maison. At the entrance she found Lucy and George, the latter high up on a ladder, with hammer and nails, arranging a curtain as directed by the former, who hastily took off her housemaid-gloves, and conducted the stranger to the Visitors' Room. There her bright face struck Mrs. Hunter with pleasant surprise, as, glancing at her watch, she said softly, "In ten minutes exactly our children will all be in school. We do not begin till eleven. May I ask you to wait here? My young carpenter must not be left to his own devices"—with a smile; "but I will return in less than ten minutes."

As, later, they passed by the corridor into the school, Mrs. Hunter boldly interrogated her guide: "Do you teach? Are you not much too young? And Lucy, with rippling cadence that suggested laughter, replied, "We all teach something—and we all learn as well—both the young and the old; Mrs. Ward even, though she is such an invalid. Oh! you must see her before you go. She wishes, I know, to hear all about your daughters; but h'sh! we must be silent now," as she threw open the schoolroom door.

An attractive spectacle met Mrs. Hunter's gaze: a large room well heated, and ventilated; the floor bare and polished; a gas fire at each end burning brightly; and abundant light from high windows, out of which children cannot see. There are pictures and maps on the walls, benches with backs of various sizes, easy-chairs for teachers, foot-stools and portable tables, a general air of comfort, and, as Mrs. Hunter entered, the stillness of studious activity.

At one end stood Mr. Cairns before a large blackboard,

with George and Harry Plimsoll, and his own child Esther beside him. A lesson in mental arithmetic was proceeding, and Lucy joined the group as soon as the visitor seated herself by Mrs. Ray's table.

Rose's group consisted of five. Percy Cairns was amongst them, and three of the children belonged to a lower social class. The table before her was covered with objects: a small globe stood by her side; a dictionary, paper, and pencil, were at hand. The little ones, ranged on the bench in front, were required every instant to rise quietly and deftly, come to the table, find and handle an object, describe it, ask questions concerning it, in some cases, point to its home on the globe, or write down its name, or look it up in the dictionary; but never did Rose, Mrs. Hunter observed, impart any knowledge of which any one of the little ones was already possessed. Rose wielded a marvellous power of unearthing from some hidden corner in a little child's brain the fact of which all were in search, and leading the entire group to rejoice at its discovery, and make its acquisition their own!

"We want them to learn," she said *sotto voce* to Mrs. Hunter, "how to teach themselves and others to think, and observe, and reason about things; to know what they do know, and where their knowledge ceases, and above all to use their knowledge altruistically." Mrs. Hunter felt puzzled by an unfamiliar word, but, true to the genius of her own upbringing, she feigned apprehension and courteous approval!

At this moment Percy came close to the two, and in an earnest stage whisper said, " Rose, do you know Lizzie Roper missed that nice voyage on Monday amongst all the islands in the Caribbean Sea ? Her mother required her to go a message, because baby was cutting a tooth, and Lizzie knows nothing at all about Trinidad! May I take her that voyage this afternoon? and go on the map, you know, the *large* map? Please say yes."

"You may, Percy—yes," Rose replied, "and be very exact. Describe well the climate and everything else, and not too fast. You remember what I told you about taking in new ideas? It is not easy, and Lizzie's brain must not be hurried and worried. Give her time, be patient— every teacher has to be patient."

"I will try, Rose; I want to be kind and good to Lizzie, and I like so much to teach."

About twelve o'clock Rose's pupils had a run in the garden, preliminary to a drawing lesson, and Rose for the moment was free.

"That boy is your brother, I presume?" said Mrs. Hunter. "Oh no! but my comrade; one of the little companions of my home."

"Indeed! Then you don't think it necessary"—this was said timidly—"to teach children to be respectful to their elders? He called you Rose quite familiarly!"

"Respectful? Oh yes! but not formal. Ah! I see what you are thinking of," and Rose's eyes beamed with expressive sympathy;—"that horrid old adage that used to perplex me also — 'familiarity breeds contempt'; of course it is nonsense, when humanity is not vile! Children, at least our children, are naturally free, confiding, familiar, but not forward or rude. We only strive to keep them natural, and you know we are training them to fitness for the new Social Order, when all class distinctions will be at an end——" She paused, for clearly Mrs. Hunter did not know: a look of alarm sprang into her face! Rose had an impulse to cry, in response to the look, " We are not dynamitards !" The truth was, her husband's caution occurred painfully to Mrs. Hunter. These opinions she was to beware of—" a new order," what could that mean ? And suppose the opinions were really dangerous, although Charles thought not; this sweet, frank creature—are her feet entangled in some diabolical snare ?

Strange to say, she never thought of her children at this moment : her emotion was purely generous ; her womanly heart yearned over Rose as she gazed in her face with knitted brow.

Rose had one of her rapid flashes of insight. She knew that this hitch in their intercourse could not be wrestled with ; it must simply be ignored. "Come and see our modellers," she said ; and led Mrs. Hunter to the farther end of the room. " They can go to the garden if they like, but you see they are too much engrossed with their work !"

Four children in smock frocks, three boys and one girl, were surrounded by figures and a few other objects of art, each child intent on reproducing in clay the object immediately before him. The eldest, a fine-looking boy of fourteen, was appealed to again and again as the ladies stood there. " Look here, Jim, the lip of my jar won't go right." "That arm, Jim! Surely the curve is wrong ?"

In a low voice Mrs. Hunter inquired : " Is that boy the teacher ?" And Rose explained : " These three—not that other boy—are children of an artist, whose wife is in bad health. He has taken her to the Riviera for the winter, and left the little ones in our charge. The artistic sense is in all of them, and we are careful to let it develop freely. No one, unless asked, interferes with their work ; but when an object is completed, it is then submitted to criticism, and if the young worker perceives and himself acknowledges the defects pointed out, he alters or destroys it, and tries again. But if not, the work is carefully pre-served for his own criticism at a further stage of his development."

Whilst speaking thus, Rose had been leading Mrs. Hunter into the garden, where old Mr. Ray was weeding a pathway. She now introduced them and returned to the school.

Mr. Ray had a keen enjoyment in showing to a visitor the strong points of the communal agricultural industry, and discoursing on the aptitude of children for floricul-ture and other open-air labour. No cabbages in the dis-trict, he firmly believed, could compare with those grown at La Maison; and Mrs. Hunter presently found herself rejoicing with the genial old man that Lotta and Blanche would be fed, if they dined there, on home-grown potatoes! It was not a matter of thought, but of feeling, that some counterbalance to the drawback of dangerous opinions lay in the general soundness of their vegetables!

On re-entering the schoolroom she perceived that a re-construction of classes had occurred.

Mr. Cairns' fresh group embraced two of the artist's children and his own boy Percy. The latter, on her approach, signalled a welcome with a speaking glance of his eye, and volunteered in a whisper the information: "Papa is teaching us science." Mrs. Hunter did not benefit by the hint. To most minds, and certainly to hers, the word "science," so used, conveys little definite meaning. What she heard was, of atmospheric conditions, the nature of the air, sun's heat, etc.; of conservation of energy, of the mutual relations of light, sound, and so on.

Must Lotta and Blanche be taught this stuff, she thought. I never was taught it—and what is the use?

Besides, when will there be time for their music and dancing, their German and French? The cloud of distrust that had lifted a little in the garden, settled down once more to depress her maternal heart. Is anything in nature more pathetic than the tender, timid fears of a mother, who tends to stand still in a rapidly moving age? Oh! the pangs she endures when her children press eagerly forward in vital streams of progress; her impotent efforts to hold them back; her confusion of mind; her bewailings over the breach, ever widening, between her own thoughts and feelings and those of her children—poor innocent, frightened mother birds!

All hail! to the good time, fast approaching, when evolution forces will no longer throw out of touch parental and filial natures; but all, in a deep, broad family life, itself progressive, will buoyantly advance with the tides of civilisation, and from first to last hold one another in a sacred, sympathetic embrace!

The dose of science that made poor Mrs. Hunter feel sick at heart was forgotten when Lucy appeared at her side and said, " Would you like now to come with me into the house and see Mrs. Ward and our baby? "

" Oh, yes! " she replied; and the moment the school was left behind, she eagerly asked, " Is music paid proper attention to here? My children should practise two hours every day."

" Indeed! " said Lucy; " then they have the gift. I am glad. My sister Rose has a great gift in music. I have none—to produce it I mean; but I can enjoy it now. It is delightful when Rose and Miss José and Esther play to us in the evenings, and Joe Ferrier sings. At home I hated music. Mother made us all learn—even the boys! Oh! such dreadful piano strumming went on all day, and one heard it all over the house! Here, it is good music only one hears, and at times when one is free to listen and enjoy.

"Practising is done in this room." She softly opened the double doors, and allowed Mrs. Hunter to look in. Esther and Vera were at the piano; a music lesson was going on. Mrs. Hunter felt comforted.

"The walls of this room," whispered Lucy, "are deafened, the piano is not heard outside; I never practise," she continued, as they pursued their way, glancing *en route* at the work-shop, the sewing-room, the library, the laboratory, and finally ascending the staircase. "Our Education Committee decided that for me to go on learning music would be a mistake—a mere waste of time. I am so glad; and it has made me love it instead of hating it. Now for our baby!" She flung open a door, revealing a large room, where instantly a beautiful girl turned round from a table and faced Lucy placing her finger to her lips. "Is baby asleep?"

"Yes" said Ruth," he has been naughty, the dear little man! I had to put him in prison, and he cried so long that now he sleeps soundly, from pure fatigue."

A baby in prison! Mrs. Hunter was bewildered; she gazed with suspicion round the room and into Ruth's expressive face. No sign of dementia appeared there; but neither in the room was there sign of a cradle, where an infant could be asleep! Lucy came to the rescue. "A stranger will never guess, Ruth, where the dear little man is hidden!" On tiptoe she advanced; Mrs. Hunter following, to what appeared to the latter a tall, rather clumsy basket for soiled linen, which stood, strange to say, in a prominent position near the fireplace.

Behold! in its depths lay a cherub boy, attitude and

breathing indicative of profound repose; one chubby
arm flung over his head, the rounded cheeks flushed, the
limbs half outstretched in soft curves, and wherever
gravitation drew the tender flesh to the basket, there,
were feathers and down to make it the softest of nests.
Mrs. Hunter laughed gently and exclaimed, "What a
darling!" and Lucy responded, "Yes, isn't he a duck!
But he is very wilful, and he must be trained to obedience,
you know; so he is often in prison, and cries himself to
sleep; but it is so nice that we need never scold him; the
dear little fellow has never once heard an angry word." *

The child did not awake, and Mrs. Hunter turned with
interest to Ruth, who stood at her table, cutting out small
garments. "Excuse me continuing my work," she said
politely to the stranger, "our little one grows fast, and
the children have asked leave to make his new clothes
themselves. I promised to have them ready in the
sewing-room to day at half-past three."

"You all seem to claim the baby," Mrs. Hunter remarked. "You are not the mother, I fancy. Is his
own mother not jealous?"

Tears welled into Ruth's eyes and she hastily lowered
them. It was Lucy who answered—"His own mother is
dead, but indeed you are right: we all feel like mothers
to him, don't we, Ruth?" And as they proceeded to Mrs.
Ward's parlour—"Ruth has lost her mother, and seen such
a lot of trouble! She is very sensitive, but we love her
dearly, and hope she will soon be quite happy with us."
She paused, rapped at a door, then entered, in response to
a cheerful "Come in;" and meanwhile an old lady, seated

* For the system of nursery training applied in La Maison, the
reader is referred to Scientific Meliorism, page 370.

with back to the intruders, was saying earnestly, "If only my Dick would marry and settle down at home! You are blessed indeed to have Vera and her husband with you always. How I envy you! It is dreadful for a mother to be bereft of her children—to be left all ——"

The sentence broke off abruptly: Mrs. Ward on her couch, had stretched out her hand to a stranger, saying, "I am glad to see you. This is my friend, Mrs. Oswald."

For the next half-hour there was confidential talk about Lotta and Blanche. To inspire confidence and draw forth expression of secret care was a peculiar quality of Mrs. Ward's temperament. Mrs. Hunter yielded readily to the influence. Her conscientious desire to do the best for her children; her personal ignorance of true education; her doubts in regard to her husband's guidance; her approval of much she had seen in La Maison; her bewilderment concerning much; her childlike readiness nevertheless to risk all, and hand over Lotta and Blanche, if only they would use the shibboleth of her faith and say they were Christians;—all this was apparent to Mrs. Ward's intellect, and touching to her feelings.

A word here and there of delicate sympathy conveyed to Mrs. Hunter the impression that she was understood; and that alone is a marvellous solace to depressed humanity. Mrs. Ward was scrupulous not to imply agreement—unanimity of sentiment or thought; yet her visitor took leave serene and cheerful, and on her way homewards pondered with inward delight some words Mrs. Ward had spoken. To her heart these words carried comfort, although to her mind they were vague, nay, obscure! "Religion," said Mrs. Ward, "will never die out of the world, I feel sure of that. It is dogma—theological dogma the age rejects! We want the young generation to beat out its creeds for itself, but we will inspire it from day to day with vital, practical religion. Our children's Ideals will be noble! worthy! and their young lives they will make conformable."

On the Monday following Mrs. Hunter's visit, Lotta and Blanche were under the roof of La Maison in a state of suppressed excitement; the change of school was a momentous novelty to them.

On Saturday of the same week a General Council was called, to hear the report of the Education Committee on the new scholars, and decide the question of their admission.

"In reference," Walter Cairns began, "to our great aim of moulding humanity to a superior type by a modern system of training, these children do not promise *much*. The father is an unmitigated Philistine (I use the term in Matthew Arnold's sense—I think you understand?); the mother is a gentle, timid, pious woman; ignorant, and, I fear, narrow. The elder girl is already too old to alter fundamentally under the play of new external forces, and in her the father's nature predominates: but the younger, Blanche, is of finer material; a more hopeful subject in every way. She has a sweet, affectionate disposition, and I think her intellect—I mean her powers of reasoning,— although as yet not active, are superior to her mother's.

"She is only ten. She has lived, I fancy, in sensations and emotions—a simple child-like existence—the intellect latent; for, clearly, the vulgar ideas and instincts that Lotta exhibits, have no hold upon her."

Mr. Spiers and Rose followed with remarks that showed the new-comers had been closely observed and studied.

After Rose, Frank, her husband, had a word to say. "These vulgar ideas of Lotta's may prove a grave danger

L

to us. Is this not so? We are pledged to the principle of no coercion, no punishment. Our children, at present, are mentally wholesome and sweet: but a little leaven— bad leaven in this case—might leaven the lump."

" Oh! Frank! you are two biological," cried Margaret, with a sparkling eye, significant for the moment of her high-bred warrior ancestors preparing for combat and con- quest, " such a figure. as that misleads! And if vulgar ideas were germs they must find a habitat—a soil to take hold in! But vulgar ideas are forces, nothing more. We shall overbear them with forces that are strong and good; and that without friction, without coercion! False ideas are subdued by the true. We simply ignore all vulgarity."

On the side of admitting the children, and trusting that Blanche would develop favourably in the school, and Lotta do it no harm, Mrs. Ward and others spoke briefly, and the vote taken later decided the matter thus: but on leaving the council chamber, Frank and Margaret returned to the charge on the subject of biological analogies!

They withdrew together to the Conversation Room, and there exercised dialectical skill in an animated, brilliant debate.

CHAPTER XI.

UNSELFISH LOVE.

FROM the memorable day when two little tear-drops in Rose Karrattray's eyes attracted his attention, Frank's emotional life had been quickened. Previous to that it was in abeyance to the intellectual side of his nature, which had strongly and rapidly developed under scientific training. His relation with Rose was as the opening of flowers to the sun, in the sweetest of meadows, in the fresh spring time; and when, after months of intercourse a mutual spontaneous impulse brought their lips together, and the kiss was given that sealed their eternal union, Frank, had the spirit of poetry been his familiar, rather than the stiff backbone of science, would have breathed in the ear of his love these well-known lines:

> " Nothing in the world is single ;
>   All things, by a law divine,
>   In one another's being mingle—
>   Why not I with thine ?"

It was true that just as:

> " The fountains mingle with the river,
>   And the rivers with the ocean, as
>   The winds of heaven mix for ever
>   With a sweet emotion,"

so these two natures had combined; and the marriage,

147   L—2

which shortly after took place was, so far as the mental constitution is concerned, merely the conscious, public recognition of a process already accomplished by the driving forces of life which lie deep below the surface, and for the most part operate unconsciously.

When their life together began in La Maison there was no tendency to selfish isolation. Their conjugal happiness lay at the roots of their being, a hidden source of perpetual joy that transfigured the ordinary aspect of existence, and fitted them to meet even humdrum duties with—exaltation?—at least with cheerful alacrity. But humdrum is not a term that applies to any duties of life in a well organised Unitary Home; and in La Maison, during the process of organisation, there was novelty, freshness, variety, and a constant call for personal effort that left no room for dulness or stupidity.

It was well for Frank that his office-work was somewhat monotonous. It left his energies unimpaired; and day after day, on his return from town, he flung himself with eager delight into every occupation that ministered in any way to the happiness or welfare of the inmates of his home.

In her "Daniel Deronda," George Eliot contrasts the unemotional intellect that "may carry us into a mathematical dreamland where nothing is but what is not," with the emotional intellect characterized by a passionate vision of possibilities, "the more comprehensive massive life feeding theory with new material." Now Frank's more comprehensive massive life had as yet simply given a human direction to his science. The latter had absorbed him at one time; now it is the application of it to human service that absorbs him.

Every discovery of how his theoretic knowledge and

mechanical skill lightens labour or promotes comfort in La Maison fills him with manly pleasure, and meanwhile the purely speculative side of his intellect is quiescent.

"Did you ever hear, ma'am, our Scotch saying—'My daughter is my daughter all her life; my son is my son till he gets a wife'?" asked old Mr. Ray of Mrs. Ward. "I find it a slander upon our sex. Frank married is more attentive to his old dad than Frank single!" and truly there had been moments when the eager scientist had felt his father a little tedious and prosy, whereas with Rose enshrined in his heart a diffusive tenderness permeated his whole nature, and softened every relation of life.

Moreover, his father and he had wider mutual interests than ever before. The domestic concerns of their bachelor abode in Liverpool Frank had cared nothing about; but here it was different, and when in conclave upon some point of difficulty, the old man would aptly produce his experience of communal life at New Lanark, and reveal by his memories of the past how pure was the flame of youthful enthusiasm for humanity enkindled by Robert Owen, his son's bosom glowed afresh with filial reverence and love.

Personal affinities are certain to declare themselves in a unitary home. The bonds of affection and links of connection will form freely in adaptation to individual natures, and as these are distinctive and richly varied, so the subjective emotional relations are bound to be equally diverse.

Frank had no consciousness of this. His comrades, exclusive of his wife and father, seemed all alike charming. He worked in joyful alacrity indiscriminately with all, and, when recreation was the business of the moment, he could romp with the boys, frolic with the girls, listen with

marital pride to his wife discoursing sweet music, take
part in whist or other games, or with Margaret and Mons.
Martin in dialectical skirmish—playful repartee,—and
feel that enjoyment equally characterised all. Mrs. Plimsoll
from the first proclaimed a special friendship with him.
In contrast with Monsieur Martin, he delightfully corro-
borated her theory of the superiority of the English over
the French: "Monsieur Martin might be clever, but
Frank was clever and practical." In household dilemmas
his cleverness proved of use; and she frequently begged
her sons to grow up like Frank, and assured them in
that case she would find " no fault."

There was one little coterie within the general group
where Frank had no footing. Miss José and Margaret,
Mr. Spiers and Henri Martin might be called the nucleus
of the communal body. In them socialism was inherent.
It was a necessity of their natures as well as an exquisite
pleasure afforded by their domestic proximity, to have
earnest discussion on the principles of their economic
faith and its wide application to human life. Mrs. Ward,
Walter Cairns, Mr. Ray, and Rose, occasionally joined
these impromptu debates, but Frank never; he was living
a simple sensational life of innocent enjoyment without
moral strain, and with his speculative faculty in abeyance.

The first change that occurred was when Ruth appeared
on the scene. The tone of exuberant life around her was
too high pitched for the girl whose spirits and health were
depressed by misfortune. She ached for comparative
solitude without loneliness, and to Rose, who attracted
her strongly, a gentle petition was often addressed.
" Could we be together alone to-day? Just a little
while, please, when the work is done ? " " Take her out,
keep her out," Dr. Basil exhorted on behalf of his patient

and there were long summer evenings when Rose and Ruth sat apart in the garden, and Frank generously relinquished his wife's society and occupied himself elsewhere.

"Come, Margaret," he said, on one of these occasions, "George and I are going to the Lab.; I have a combustion on; will you join us? I know you have studied chemistry."

"Oh, Frank! I should like it above everything," Margaret cried, with a happy light in her eyes, "I do so want to know if your knowledge is very much greater than mine. But wait just a moment, pray do; I must run and tell Miss José where I shall be."

Margaret's chemistry was much further advanced than Frank had anticipated. A month hence the two were engaged on original research in a hidden department of nature's operations, the circuitous intricacies of which were known to themselves only under the roof of La Maison. Frank's scientific enthusiasm revived, and this time the human element was not absent! He would stay his hand to admire the neatness and delicacy of Margaret's manipulations, the precision of her adjustments. Her facile intellect, too, surprised and delighted him. His own power of concentration, no doubt, was greater than hers; but her keenness of insight, her suggestive imagination, the rapidity of her concepts, her mental combinations, and her passage from one set of conditions to another— "They are marvellous," said Frank to himself, and so he told Rose; but when he tried to place before the latter Margaret's exploits, on a chemical background of which she knew nothing, the effect was disappointing! Rose could not admire with enthusiasm what she did not understand, and her husband instinctively ceased to be confidential and communicative on the subject of laboratory work.

In that mysterious region, "the Lab.," there was sometimes an experiment in progress of entrancing interest to the amateur chemists, and Frank's mind resumed an old habit of occasional abstraction from immediate surroundings, to grapple with a problem whose ultimate solution depended on practical demonstration.

The temptation to abstraction was imminent when music was going on. He had no inherited love for music, and his pride in his wife's admirable gift had lost the freshness of novelty. Hence it frequently happened that Frank's eyes in the music-room roved in search of Margaret's with the inquiry—how was her mental part engaged?

A quick understanding between the two was established. To both, their fellowship in work became a source of keen and lasting enjoyment.

The summer was gone and winter well advanced, when Margaret gave Frank a great surprise. " I am going to give up chemistry," she said; "I have only been waiting till this work was completed, and now you are sending results to the London Society; so this, Frank,' her voice sounded a little doleful, "is my last appearance in the Lab."

Frank looked at her with a face of blank disappointment. "Do you not like it, Margaret?" he said, "I thought you did."

" Like it ! " she cried, " why I like it too much; that is the reason I mean to give it up." She paused; a sense of relief had brought a smile to Frank's lips, and Margaret felt hurt. " Do you think I am not in earnest?" she asked, and looked at him with flushing cheeks and eyes that slowly filled with tears. "I am doing what it is painful to do, because it is right."

"What makes it right?" cried Frank in a playful tone, while, at the moment a series of mingled emotions, called forth by the tears, moved him inwardly. He recalled the mystery of Roses' tears, shed for Basil before he loved or even knew his darling; but Margaret, he thought, he knew Margaret, and loved her. "Yes, I love her," he said to himself, with a dogged feeling as though opposing forces were present; "yet I am just as much shut out here as there from the secret of those tears.—Can it be that the world's paltry standards of propriety are interfering between us somehow?" and a wave of devotion to Margaret, and anger with some hidden enemy swept over him.

The next instant Margaret was speaking and Frank listening in a purely intellectual though combative mood. "I am not like you, Frank," she began, "a scientist pure and —— "

"You are better than I," he laughed back to her. "Those fine fingers of yours —— "

"Be serious," she checked him impatiently. "Try to see what I mean. The temperament of science, there I fail I am keen, I am too impetuous. Now, don't tell me that is the fault of my sex, and no woman should study science."

"Fault! It is no fault," exclaimed Frank. "It is a charm of your sex, if you like." A reproachful glance made him hasten to add, "but I am quite in the dark! If you love any science, if you are keen and impetuous in its pursuit, why not pursue it? My caution, remember, well balances your haste, our results are to be trusted."

"Oh! I know that. It is not results—at least, I mean not objective ones, but the subjective results,—I am afraid of." As her words came with difficulty, Margaret's face so clearly expressed her earnest wish to explain, that the combative mood in her companion gave way to a sympathetic one. "Have you neglected any duties for chemistry?" he asked gently.

"Not in the letter, but in the spirit I have. I am introspective, you know: you are not. That is why it is difficult for you to understand. My love for the physical science has grown to a passion of late, and my human life is hurt by it. I mean, my human interests have become less important to me. That cannot be right! At least, I will give up science at present, and perhaps ——"

"Well, dear Margaret," said Frank, interrupting her, "I dare not interfere with so delicate a matter as a woman's conscience, though I don't understand your ·scruples: but look here! you are compelling me to a sacrifice also! You know that, don't you? I shall hate the very look of the Lab.," — and he glanced around as they stood, "without your presence. I could not work here without you. Am I, too, then to give up original research? Is that fair to the world? And when we, in La Maison, are doubly bound to promote scientific progress?" Margaret's look of astonishment made him hastily add, "You must face all the facts when you take a step like this."

Her surprise gave way to anger as she answered him quickly, "It is you, Frank, who are unfair! I am not the arbiter of your life, surely? Besides, how absurd! Why, you must be a poor creature indeed, if your work for the world, for humanity, depends wholly on female co-operation!"

The anger had disappeared, an arch look betokened the intention to rally him further, when a chink of the door was opened and Mrs. Plimsoll's head—she was in too hot haste apparently to enter—became visible. "Can you help me, Frank Ray?" she said, breathlessly: "the cistern begins to freeze, it must be seen to at once. The Frenchman is there, but I leave you to guess if he —— " Her sentence broke off; Frank had promptly opened the door, and the two passed hurriedly through the hall and ascended the staircase together.

On that evening—it was a Saturday, and the chemical research had been completed in the afternoon—Frank had many fits of abstraction. He did not seek Margaret's society again; nevertheless she, her thoughts and feelings, and not combinations of elementary gases and fluids, formed the pieces of his intellectual puzzle. The next day, after a long walk with Rose, whilst the latter lay down to rest, he went in search of Margaret. Her taunt of unmanliness in his renunciation of chemistry when deprived of female co-operation had wounded his vanity, although he had not much, and he was armed to the teeth with arguments in self defence! But he might have spared himself the trouble of forging these implements of intellectual warfare. His antagonist had changed her attitude, and proclaimed it at once with feminine nonchalance: " You were right, Frank, to feel you should give up original research as well as I. I could not get you out of my thoughts last night."

Frank smiled; it was pleasant to know she was thinking of him when he had been thinking of her. "I said, rudely, I was not arbiter of your life, surely; but we must all partake of one another's lives, and I was wrong to decide on my own action without a glance at the result of that action on you."

They were in the corridor, and suddenly she turned towards the library, saying, " Come with me, do; there is a passage in 'The Old Order Changes' that haunts me. I must find it, I want you to see it."

Five minutes later they were seated, with a volume open before them, in the Conversation-room. "Miss Consuelo Burton is speaking. Ah yes! Here is the picture;" and Margaret, placing her finger on the page, read aloud: "'I used once to go to lectures at the Royal Institution, and arriving one night at the door, I saw, through a lower window, two professors discussing what apparently was a fossil. I see their faces now—grand, intellectual faces, full of what I suppose it is right to call elevation. And just outside, only a few paces away from them, were two cabmen, quarrelling over a pot of beer. What two different worlds were these, side by side; and what good did the higher do the lower?'" Margaret lifted her eyes from the book and looked at Frank, "Your face is grandly intellectual," she said, "when some difficult problem has you in its grip; it got mixed up in my dream, with these two professors! I awoke this morning with a curious conviction that somehow it rested with me to turn your powers in a new direction."

"Oh! the cabman direction, I suppose."

Margaret took no notice of this flippant observation; she returned to the volume, and resumed reading: "'I shall never again feel, till I learn how to work for others, that it is more than solemn child's-play to be feathering my own spiritual nest.' You and I, Frank, shut up in that Lab. together, have been feathering our nest. To me the enjoyment was simply intense."

"And if we had hated the work, I presume you would have continued it. Bah! Margaret, you provoke me," cried Frank. "You said yesterday your temperament is not scientific. No, indeed, it is not! It is religious, and of an antiquated type! You are an ascetic pure and simple."

This attack was received with a heightened colour, but

the reply came gently, " My temperament is irrelevant to our question at present, which is a general one, not individual. Another time," with a smile, " you may pull me to pieces, Frank, but not now. The problem before us is this : At the present epoch of social life, what do we stand in need of most ? Is it discovery of new truth in the physical sciences ? My answer is, No ; and I am prepared to overwhelm you with logical proof that that answer is correct ! The pressing need is for guidance in action, and in that work our best scientific intellects ought to be absorbed, unless some special hindrance exists—which is not your case. This guiding action, it has been well said, is really the supreme function of science in human life.

" You have shown me a new thing, a marvellous thing, dear Frank,— the strength and power of a single, clear, scientific, masculine intellect. Applied in any direction, it must accomplish much. It has made plain, even to my feeble sight, the most fascinating pictures of the labyrinth of nature ; but I tell you frankly," and she lifted her eyes to her companion and spoke with a moral enthusiasm that suddenly enkindled a like spark in him, " I long to see it searching strenuously, ardently for the Ariadne-like thread which, placed in the hands of Humanity, will guide it through that labyrinth. We shall not find that clue in the Lab.! believe me."

For fully an hour their conversation continued, and when they separated, Frank was committed to a new enterprise—the scientific examination of social economics.

His leisure time for the next few weeks was dedicated to varied reading,—varied, not in respect of the subject-matter, but of the different sources from which it was drawn. The Ricardo and Mill views of wealth and the laws of our commercial system were already familiar to

him, but the new light thrown here and there on the
vast, the baffling complexity of social industry from the
lamps of Sismondi, Comte, Carlyle, Ruskin, Marx, Gron-
lund, Lester Ward, and Carruthers, Margaret was resolute
he should perceive ; and to please her he carefully studied
every passage to which she referred him.

An interruption occurred when the birth of Frank's
child took place. For some days economics were entirely laid aside. Devotion to Rose and the new-comer
filled his spare moments, but there was no separation
from Margaret. She and Vera shared the nursing, by
appointment of the Committee, and many little spurts of
social science talk, when Rose was in a condition to enjoy
it, burst forth in the invalid's room.

Rose was healthy, although not muscular ; her recovery
was without drawback ; and the time soon came when,
reclining on a sofa, her infant in her arms, she herself invited an immediate return to the economic studies.

She had rejoiced heartily when Frank disclosed the change
in his scientific inquiries. Of chemistry she knew nothing, whilst in the field of Sociology she had long been
a deeply interested inquirer. It was natural that she
should feel glad when her husband's mind turned from
the physical science, that was all mystery, to enter a
region whither hers could occasionally follow. Till now
she had never beheld him at work with Margaret. At
play she had seen them often together. A new knowledge
of her husband's intellect and acquirements broke upon
her. In discussion with Margaret, his speculative faculty
showed all its vigour, his reasoning powers their full
swing. If they differed, all his resources were required to
meet his opponent's dialectical thrusts ; if they agreed,
their minds in unison would seize in masterly style the

abstract, the ethereal, and, to use a Carlylean phrase, condense it, to take shape and body.

Miss Consuelo Burton's reflection became Rose's as she gazed: grand intellectual faces, these, full of elevation; and at rare moments when the terms on their lips were not production, wealth, capital, profit, loss, rent, and such-like, but the People, their unceasing toil, their immeasurable degradation, Margaret would breathe forth her passionate vision of possibilities, and Frank, with intellect become emotional, would respond in the deep, the generous tones of lofty religion—the religion of humanity.

To listen, admire, and join the discussion, when she could, was the first phase of Rose's condition, and the second was like unto it; only she listened more and talked less. But by and by an uneasy sensation—was it jealousy?—created a change. She observed with the eye more keenly than before, while the ear was dulled to the finer issues of debate. Once Margaret, turning to her for sympathy and aid, found her eyes full of mingled absence and pain. "O, Frank!" she cried, hurriedly, "we have tired her too much; we must be silent now." Then gently smoothing her pillow, "Lie down, dear, and rest," she said; "we did not mean to be selfish, but strength is so apt to forget weakness."

"Will you tell me, Margaret," Rose asked of her faithful nurse, in a mood of confidential intercourse, when the two were alone together, "how comes it that you are not married? No man whom you loved could resist your attractions. Have you never loved?"

"No, never," she answered simply, "I knew no one of the opposite sex whose presence thrilled me as Miss José's did, or with whom I would have cared to live. O, Rose! is it not wonderful how happy we are here. I love

every one under this roof; and you know, dear, I was really
in danger of my heart becoming atrophied or fossilised, or
something, in that dreary, hateful mansion at Leeds.
There was nothing important to do there and nothing to
love. Oh, I shudder to think of it."

Rose drew down her head and deliberately gave her lips
a kiss that was like a consecration of their friendship.
"How sweet is your nature," Margaret was again speaking,—"the hardness of mine you will never understand.
But riches, the surroundings of luxury and pride from the
cradle, you have escaped these, darling Rose." A whimper
from the cradle at their side claimed attention. The
infant was raised in Margaret's arms, and fondled, as she
crooned in her ears; "and you too, my pet, you too will
escape."

When Rose's strength was restored, and she had resumed household duties, the economic studies advanced
rapidly, but without her presence. Some excuse for
leaving the students to themselves was ever ready. The
children, or Ruth, or her own babe required her; failing
these, her music could no longer be neglected, and
she would hurry to the music-room, and with soul
absorbed in the grand strains of Handel or Mozart,
she found the personal element drop out of her feeling,
and ceased for the moment to remember Margaret and
Frank.

Their little one was two and a half months old when
Rose told Frank that she wished to visit her parents in
Devonshire, and make them acquainted with their grand-
daughter. A recent writer tells us that the normal
woman's life, supporting an elaborately cumbrous
domestic machine upon her shoulders, is full of care
and weariness. Now, in our Unitary Home the domestic

machinery, although elaborate, cumbers no one. The occasional absence of members, whether on a call of duty or pleasure, is foreseen and provided for without any breach in the general comfort. Frank only waited for his own weekly holiday, to convey his wife and child to the south.

A day in Devonshire in spring, sweet hyacinths and bright blossoms everywhere, and the breath of summer in the air! Who can resist such influences? A sombre mood in which young Mrs. Ray had indulged of late, disappeared. She was bright and frolicsome as in the days of their honeymoon, which, said Frank, but for this imp—and he proudly held out to her the smiling little one,—I would think has come back to us. "Look here, dear," he said, when he bade her adieu, "these cheeks, since baby was born, have reminded me of a pale lily, and not of my Rose. The native air will work wonders, if you are not impatient. Take care to come back to me my rose-coloured Rose. I shall miss you sadly; but, thank goodness, I have Margaret, and the matter in hand with her now—did she tell you?—is synthesis, not analysis: a scheme for employing our surplus fund to the best intent. What a grand creature she is! Don't you think so?" And Rose, as her husband jumped into the carriage, replied, "I do —yes, I do." As the train moved off he looked from the window; she smiled and bowed, but her cheeks, he observed with surprise, had suddenly blanched.

Four weeks later the postman at the Rectory gate handed Rose a letter. "Not from Frank, but from Basil," she murmured, and hastened to read it in her chamber alone by her sleeping babe. The letter ran thus :—

"Dear Rose,—In the name of wonder, what makes you linger so long with the old people?

M

" Frank is devoting himself to Margaret; and, by George! I would do the same if Emma forsook me as you do him. La Maison is not like a bachelor-lodging; and husbands—well, they are no more stocks and stones than other men. I can say no more. But come home at once, and don't mention this hint.—Your affectionate brother, BASIL.—P. S. A little accident last night. Margaret's dress caught fire; she is not hurt to speak of, but the fright Frank was in ——. That showed me how the wind lay; he is in love or on the verge of falling in love. I hate to write this, but, come home."

Rose did not appear in the drawing-room that evening.

"She lies quite still, with her eyes closed, poor dear; her headache must be very bad," Mrs. Karrattray said to the Rector, after a visit upstairs; and he replied, "I fear she is reading too much at night; I see she has George Herbert's poems, and a volume of Milton out of my library: and poetry, you remember, made her always forget time."

But the volume of Milton at that moment under Rose's pillow was scarcely corroborative of the Rector's theory. Would he have recognised the old poet's quaint words had he heard them, as he might have done at the moment, issuing faintly from his daughter's pale lips ?

"' What a calamity is this! What a sore evil under the sun ! . . . some conscionable and tender pity . . . for those who have unwarily, in a thing they never practised before, made themselves the bondmen of a luckless and helpless matrimony.' O Frank ! my darling, my darling." Rose stirred uneasily, in a paroxysm of anguish: "my heart is full of tender pity; you are not to blame !" Then, quoting again from old Milton, as though the words soothed her grievous pain, "' For all the wariness that can be used, it may yet befall a discreet man to be mistaken in his choice.' "

There was no sleep for Rose that night, and perhaps it was well that the little one fretted and demanded much tending at the hands of its gentle mother. Towards morning she was pacing the room, the child in her arms, and over and over again repeating to herself, " ' Better to have loved and lost than never to have loved at all.' Ah ! Winnie, my treasure, mine always," she suddenly wailed. "Your face will remind him he loved me once, me only."

For two days little Winnie was ill, and all the inmates of the Rectory were deeply concerned.

To Basil's telegram "When do you return ?" Rose bade her mother reply, "Not at once," nothing more, and added; " dear Frank must not be alarmed; I shall write to him." But she delayed, and her husband kept silence.

On the fourth morning, however, came a note : it was meagre for him—"Dear Rose, what is this Basil tells me ? You will not come home ! He asked you to come ! I don't understand; why did he do that? Is anything wrong? write at once to your husband. I am miserable. FRANK."

Rose took up her pen and began, then faltered, paused, tore up the sheet, and on a fresh one wrote hurriedly : "Dear Margaret—I grieved to hear of your accident; I hope you no longer suffer from it. Tell Frank I shall come home by and by. Winnie was ill, but she is better now. He need not be the least uneasy. Yours and his lovingly, ROSE."

The next day, towards evening, a traveller, weary and dust-stained, looked in at the Rectory window. " Oh, Frank ! I am so glad to see you," cried Mrs. Karrattray;

M—2

"all are out except Rose, and she is upstairs. Shall I call her?"

"No, no; how is the child?" he asked anxiously, and then, with a cautious step, he ascended the staircase.

In a room where the rays of the setting sun still lingered, Rose, her hands uplifted, was playing with Winnie. In an instant her waist was encircled by a strong arm, and in silence her husband gazed into her face. No roses were there, and the pallor deepened as the tender eyes responded to his with the timid wistfulness of yearning love. When the kiss came, it was with hysteric violence. His lips pressed hers again and again, and Rose knew it an outcome of passionate pain.

"You are tired, love," she said, "I shall get you refreshment."

His impatient "No, Rose, we must talk together first; I am sick unto death," was ignored. The calmness, the wisdom of moral strength lay on her side; he yielded, and all that evening, as he lay back on his easy-chair in the family circle—speaking little but feeling much,—his wife's sweet presence was as a new revelation to an earnest inquiring mind.

The younger couple had retired, and the elder were exchanging uneasy surmises.

"Yes," said Rose's mother, " she is often sad."

"She was always quiet," said the Rector, " but marriage has saddened her, disappointed her."

" Oh, marriage disappoints every woman ——"

" What, my dear! Do you mean to tell me that yours ——"

" Oh, I am not complaining of you, James, at all; but the position tries a woman in every way, and when the family is large ——"

"Well, Winnifred, Christian patience helps you there surely? 'Lo, children are an heritage of the Lord: and, the fruit of the womb is His reward.'"

Mrs. Karrattray's mind refused to wander from Rose. "I thought in that Communal Home she would be so free from domestic cares and worries."

"Ah! there I did not agree with you, if you remember; and depend upon it I was right. Rose is jealous. No woman can be happy who has not her husband all to herself. The thing is unnatural. I shall have to insist that Frank give Rose a home of her own." This conclusion eased the good Rector's mind, and shortly afterwards he was peacefully snoring in a room that was distant from the one occupied by Rose and Frank.

The distance was well, in respect of the sensitive motherly brain that courted sleep on the pillow beside him; for earnest impassioned talk broke the silence of night in that chamber for many hours.

"I have told you the truth, the whole truth," Frank was speaking; "I have nothing more to confess. Are you jealous? Are you angry?"

"Ah, my dearest!" Rose said, "these feelings, if I had them, are paltry, evanescent, not worth a thought at a critical moment like this: we stand at a turning-point in our lives—a crisis! Let us make no mistake."

"Do you mean to insinuate," her husband cried impetuously, an angry flash in his eyes, "that our marriage was a mistake?"

"No, it was not, thank God, it was not. Our innocent child is the offspring of a pure, a true union. There will be no discords in her nature for which we are answerable. But, Frank, darling, what *was* no mistake may become one. It may become a calamity, a sore evil under the sun—'Who sees not'"—and almost unconsciously she quoted from Milton the passage she had pondered so often : "'How much more Christianity it would be to break by divorce——'"

"Divorce! absurd, impossible!" Frank muttered between his teeth; "'that which is more broken by undue and forcible keeping, rather than that the whole worship of a man's life should languish and fade away beneath the weight of an immeasurable grief and discouragement.'"

"Frank! Frank! if your life languishes, if your happiness is dimmed by your union with me, O! my love, it would kill me; I should die of grief." And flinging herself on her knees by his side, Rose hid her face on his shoulder.

He bent down; then holding her in a close embrace, he whispered hoarsely, "I swear, Rose, I give you my word as an honest man, my heart *is* with you. I have not known it, perhaps, rightly till to-night. I know it now. My blood, my passionate instincts may swerve; my heart has never swerved. I love Margaret; what man would not? But you are my wife."

"Dear Margaret," said Rose, as she drew herself from her husband's clasp and looked earnestly in his face; "is she unhappy? tell me that. We have no right to think only of ourselves, we must think of her."

Frank sprang to his feet and paced the room with knitted brows; then pausing before his wife, he spoke with agitation in a tone half-resentful: "Margaret is a true woman, she has never, I am certain, had a thought disloyal to you; but unhappy! of course she is unhappy. That note of yours, what could she make of it? And if you insist on separating us——"

"I will never do that," said Rose, plaintively, and Frank, returning to his seat, threw his arm around her, asking gently, "You trust me again?"

Rose did not respond. She lifted a book from the table, and whilst her husband looked on surprised, quietly turned the leaves, then read to him in a calm voice: "'It is a less breach of wedlock to part with wise and quiet consent betimes, than to foil and profane that mystery of joy and union. . . It is not the outward continuing of marriage that keeps whole that covenant, but whatsoever does most according to peace and love.' I have no reproaches to make, Frank,"—and lifting her eyes, she looked steadily into his; "you had never seen her when you married me. I think her as noble as you do; she is a peerless woman! My intellect is no match for hers, but yours is; I have seen that. O, Frank! the law gives you to me, I know, as my property! I renounce the claim! I scorn it!"—her eyes flashed fire as Frank's had done a moment before;—"but I demand, in the name of our common womanhood, that you make no mistake now. By that which is purer, deeper, holier than man's laws, judge truly between us which is your wife? 'Whatsoever we do,' beloved, let it be for 'peace and love to all.'"

"If I did love Margaret best, where were my Rose's peace?" Frank asked, very tenderly; but he gave no time for reply. With a passionate caress, he whispered earnestly, "You are wrong, all wrong! dear wife; I am but a man, with all the frailties of flesh and blood. You are a saint, still we are one, indivisible; and 'let not man put asunder that which God hath joined together.'"

The Rector had no chance next day to propose his panacea for matrimonial discomforts. The young couple seemed closely united, though both looked pale and ill.

To his surprise they announced, as their mutual wish, that Rose should remain, with her child, at the Rectory, whilst Frank went abroad, if arrangements for this could be made in his office and at La Maison. In parting at this time Frank's words were: "Write to me constantly, Rose; and remember you promised to put back that book of old Milton's into the library;" and Rose, after a tender farewell, said, "My love to dear Margaret; bid her come to me as soon as she can."

A week later Frank was in Belgium; Margaret and Rose were together.

South Devonshire was an unknown country to Margaret, and this was her first holiday since she entered La Maison. "I feel like a child," she said softly to Rose, in the Rector's presence, after her first walk with him; "I am wild with delight! Those delicious lanes, that breezy upland, the distant sea and lovely little Dawlish lying at our feet—it is glorious!" The Rector was tired; he had taken up a journal, and lay back in his chair; but now he remarked, "You drove a pair of ponies formerly, Miss Dunmore, I believe; what a pity I have no pony carriage. You are an enthusiastic admirer of scenery, and ours is fine."

"Dear sir, I shall see it on foot. I am strong: you will let me explore in all directions alone? As for carriages! I would interdict them, you know, to the young. I am a Socialist, and think them a luxury to which we are not entitled, so long as our proletariat is clothed in rags and living in slums."

The Rector shook his head a little solemnly. "You young reformers want ballast! Respect for property is the very foundation of society: you want to overthrow the barriers of class distinction. Besides, 'The poor ye shall have with you always.'—But excuse me, my dear," he said courteously, " I must leave you now, and go to my study."

Fatigue was a bad preparation for argument. The Rector's caution withdrew him at this moment for the wise securing of an afternoon's nap in the strictest retirement!

Margaret traversed the country in a solitude more congenial than the company of her host, although she greatly respected the kindly old man.

Day after day she returned to Rose, brimful of health and spirits, her hands filled with ferns, wild-flowers, and geological treasures ; her tongue eager to describe all the beauties she had seen.

Nearly a week had thus elapsed before the sensitive spot in the consciousness of each was, at last, approached, and the emotional crisis that both had recently passed through freely discussed between them.

For half an hour they talked gravely, earnestly, but without excitement. Then Margaret's cheeks grew flushed as she said, " If his heart had passed from you to me I should hate him—not love him ! He would not be our Frank, the Frank I esteem as well as love. It may be true—nay, it is true that his brain and mine are cast in a similar mould, as you say : we are scientific, you are artistic. What of that ? We are many-sided creatures, bewilderingly complex. I have helped him to grow ? As if you too, dear, had not done that ! I am constantly seeing in him some quality that reminds me of Rose, as in you what reminds me of him !

" We all, unconsciously, absorb one another; our past is wrought into us and makes our to-day. In that noble, tender, unselfish dream of yours you forgot some facts patent to me. You can no more efface yourself from

Frank's entire being than I at this moment could
become you. He is essentially faithful and true. To
dislocate his past and his present were to disfigure his
life, to distort his whole nature. I repudiate, I treat with
derision that false notion that he and I, forgetting you,
could be happy together for one moment. O, Rose! dear,
how miserable this made me! I felt for a time as though
the solid happiness we had so laboriously built up were
beginning to topple down about our heads. If it had, oh!
I think, dear, I should have laid myself down under the
ruins to die! But now the danger has all passed, has
it not?—the ugly, hateful dream! We shall always be
loving, and true to one another? Is that not so?" She
rested her elbow on the table by her side, and supporting
her chin on her hand, turned to Rose the pathetic look
of a dumb animal courting a caress. But, as the latter
responded with a caressing movement the face changed.
Its expression became keenly intellectual.

"See here, Rose," she said, "Frank is not introspective,
I told him that! The absence of the quality is a danger,
a curious masculine deficiency. Men are cruelly betrayed
into unworthy deflections not from baseness of any kind,
but simply from the absence of a habit of introspection!
Don't you think so? I tell you what, dear, we shall train
our boys carefully to self-observation. I don't mean anything morbid, you know; but they ought to possess a
rational knowledge of their feelings as well as their
thoughts. Then the instincts, the senses would be
under control, whilst love—the purest, noblest love
could be always free."

That evening Margaret wrote to Miss José: "Have no
fears for my friendship with Rose: she is the sweetest of
women. Frank and I would be vile indeed could

we consciously wound her by so much as a pin's prick."

Frank's letters from Belgium, and later from Germany, were full of interest for Margaret as well as Rose. He was diligently inquiring concerning the great movement for the enfranchisement of labour in these countries; but in one letter, an enclosure—it was a simple song, not original, Frank had no gift that way—was for Rose's eye only—and carefully was it preserved by her.

> "Think not I roam afield
>   With heart untrue;
> The gifts my rambles yield
>   Are all for you.
>
> "The bird must leave her nest
>   And fledglings five,
> The honey-bee must rest
>   Far from her hive.
>
> "New regions I explore
>   While day is bright;
> My heart, with richer store,
>   Goes home at night."
>   —CONSTANCE C. W. NADEN.

CHAPTER XII.

THE CONDUCT OF LIFE.

School was over for the day, but Blanche Hunter had not yet left La Maison. The month was November, and the year 1892. She stood with Harry Plimsoll in a quiet corner of the play-room, engaged in talk that was confidential and a little depressing, to judge by the sob that caught the girl's breath more than once.

"Mother says it is vulgar and rude to talk of love—children should never do so. O, Harry! it is dreadful to feel you may not say just whatever you think to your very own mama."

"Well, dear," the boy comforted her, "I love you whether we say it or not; and it can't be wrong to say what you feel. It is only pretending to feel what you don't feel that is wrong. You are not to promise to marry me, remember that. You might come to love another man better: and a fellow has to be awfully sure he can make the girl happy. Come, Blanche, let us have a game now at Ringoal. It's awfully jolly to be together."

That evening, as eight o'clock drew near, a group of boys stood on the staircase near the door of the salon. "Stop, stop, Fred!" said Percy Cairns, arresting a boy on his way to the salon; "don't go in yet: the Criticism

Meeting begins at eight. We mayn't talk there now. Esther will tell us when Monsieur Martin ——"

"He's been to Shipley," George Plimsoll interrupted.

"Shipley! Oh! I say, George, where's that?" queried Harry.

"It's in Yorkshire, man—don't you know? A lot of fellows are out on strike there; they've been awfully exploited."

"Exploited! What's that?"

"Why, Harry, what a fellow you are for not knowing things. You should really study the catechism on Surplus Value. To exploit is, to get more than one gives in a bargain. These men have given hard work and long hours to their employers, and the employers have given them in return, as wages, you know, only a quarter of the value of their work, and kept three-quarters for themselves! Oh, it is a shame!" He took from his pocket a half-crown, and fingering it affectionately, said in a meditative tone, "They can't even pay the penny a week for their lectures just now. I'll give them this if he takes me with him to Shipley. I hope he will, and I do hope they'll let me learn how to be a Champion of the People."

"Champion? Well, if that means gabbing, George, you'll do it well."

"Shut up, Harry," said one of the artist's sons, impatiently, "gab and gabbing are low words; I've told you that before. Do let us be gentlemen, if we can."

"I can't be a gentleman altogether," said George, gravely, "I must learn a trade—a handicraft, you know; I am bound to be one of themselves, and my hands will be rough. A gentleman's hands, like yours, Jim—oh, my! what jolly clean nails!"

"Come in now," Esther called softly from the salon

door, and the boys responded. In an orderly fashion they
entered the room, and seated themselves on chairs already
placed suitably for the business of the evening.

Besides the members of the household, all of whom
were present—except the babes and two ladies, Mrs. Basil
Karrattray and Margaret, engaged in attending to them
—there were three visitors in the room, at their own
special request, and by George's gracious permission.
Yes, for George is the subject matter of the proposed
criticism. But to judge from his dauntless look as he
placed himself in a conspicuous position opposite the
chairman, the boy is not troubled with self-conscious
pangs of any description in facing the ordeal.

The chairman, Mr. Spiers, opened proceedings by asking Ruth Amor to read the minutes of the last general
council, in so far as they bore upon the business now
before them. These set forth the dicta that George
Plimsoll has been seized by a life-inspiration, and is
entitled to the aid of the Community in promotion of his
aims—the aims being sincere and worthy of respect, from
the standpoint of social morality. He wished, in his own
words, to learn plumber-work or carpentry, or both, if
that were possible; he would earn a wage by his labour,
and live on the wage, however small, like the rest; but
he wanted his mind free and well stored with knowledge
that would be useful to his comrades, the working men.

Might he give up Latin and chemistry, and even botany
and drawing in his education? He had not time for all,
and he wanted to read the whole history of the growth of
social institutions in different countries, and understand
exactly where the old political economy is wrong, and
why riches and poverty everywhere seem to grow together
side by side, as Mr. George's book shows. Then perhaps,

if he knew all these things, he could teach working men and help them to get ready for the time when they will have no masters to crush them down, the time—and every one says it must come—of the Emancipation of Labour! George ended with a somewhat ambitious petition: "Please let me be a champion of the people, and one of themselves; and please let me go with Monsieur Martin when he lectures to the people, that I may get to know them and understand what they want, and just how they feel."

Some explanatory remarks by the Chairman followed, to the effect that before the consent of the Commune could be given to the extension of George's life relations, it was desirable and important to bring under criticism his conduct in respect of already existent relations: they had therefore met to inquire into his fulfilment of domestic and personal duties, and every one, it was hoped, would speak freely and frankly on the subject. George perfectly understood that the object in view was no fault-finding or anti-social one, but simply to assist him in the formation of character and the right direction of his life.

Now begins the ordeal for George. He looked round a little uneasily, and a momentary glance at his mother betrayed where there lay a sensitive spot.

It was Mrs. Ward, however, who opened the discussion, and not in an attitude of attack.

"You are all, I hope, strangers in personal experience to the discomfort I suffer from the bouncing habits of children. It seems natural to some young people to bounce in and out of a room; to be impulsive, sudden, a little violent in their movements, and even in the tones of their voices. Now, perhaps, all old people, to whom calmness of nerve is an essential of comfort, must suffer to some extent, when in daily contact with children; and I, being an invalid, am abnormally sensitive. This consideration made me silent for a time; but when, four months ago, a Conduct Club was organised by the children themselves, I thought it my duty to write a short paper on the subject, that those of them whose sympathetic forces are already strong enough to control the physical might be in possession of facts.

"Since that time a marked difference has occurred; the skipping and bouncing, which, no doubt, are absolutely necessary ebullitions of youthful force, are kept well within bounds. I believe they are more indulged in than formerly in the garden and play-room, or wherever the outlet does not trespass on the liberty of the weak; but certainly no one of delicate nerves need now be afraid to become an inmate of La Maison.

"I bring this matter before you in reference to George, because he was distinctly one of the most boisterous, and he has proved, in this instance, that he has a nature full of kindly sympathy for his fellow-creatures, and capable of considerable self-control. I am quite of opinion that this criticism-meeting will be of use to him. He is, so far as my observation goes, a manly boy, who will patiently bear to have his faults pointed out, and perseveringly set himself to correct them."

As Mrs. Ward finished she threw a glance at George, who nodded to her lightly, as much as to say, I will.

Mrs. Plimsoll now rose to her feet, and in a slightly magisterial posture and tone, said, "George's father, my late husband, was a gentleman born. I would like my son to be a gentleman too, and neither a plumber nor carpenter. But boys are wilful, as I know to my cost; and Mr. Spiers, he says that George should be free to choose for

himself; so I will say no more about that, as here I stand.
What I do say is this: George is not a bad boy, though *I*
say it that am his mother, and praising him is like praising myself. But he is lazy of a morning, and always was;
though why he should be I don't know, for his father was
an early riser. He keeps me going back to call him, which
is a great waste of my time, not to speak of my patience.
Now Harry, he ——"

The chairman interrupted with an uplifted hand, and
"Not Harry at present, please; he is not under criticism."

"Oh! well, Mr. Chairman," Mrs. Plimsoll replied, hurriedly, "I was not going to complain of Harry, though he
has more faults than George, to my mind. George is
never rude to his mother."

This was said with a broadly significant look at Harry.
Clearly the motherly mind was bent upon extending
the sphere of these valuable operations, and gaining
some benefit by a side-wind for the more refrac-
tory son.

That young gentleman coloured up, and Mrs. Plimsoll,
aware of the fact, applied herself with renewed satisfaction
to the critical subject in hand.

"George is never rude, as I said, but he argufies more
than I like; and it is strange, for his father had no bad
habit of that sort. He used often to say, 'I will not argue
with you, Annie. If once a husband and wife begin to argue
there is no end.' But George, now—he always wants to
argue; and only yesterday, when I told him to sew a
button on his jacket, he argued about it, said it might try
his eyes to thread the needle, and the doctor had said
he would grow short-sighted if he tried his eyes. Just as
if short-sighted people had not buttons to sew on as well
as others! and, to my certain knowledge, that button is

N

not sewed on now. I call that disobedience, but here there are different names for most things.

"It vexes me all the more, because if there is a rule better than another within this Home, it is that the boys have to darn their own stockings and sew on their own buttons. As to these criticisms, I do not know, I am sure; but I shall think well of this one if it makes George sew on that button and get up prompt when I call him of a morning."

Mrs. Plimsoll sat down, her little self-conscious smile betokening that she conceived she had acquitted herself creditably in a difficult position.

Mr. Cairns was the next speaker.

"This laziness in the morning," said he,—"and I have observed that George is sometimes only half alive in his first working hour of the day—may prove a serious drawback, a stumblingblock in his path. Health may be partly the cause, and Dr. Basil just now pays special attention to his physical condition; but inertia yielded to, grows upon one, and George must learn to struggle manfully with it as against a bad habit. If his health requires an unusual amount of sleep, he should go to bed early.

"It is clearly our social duty, when a personal disability demands sacrifice somewhere, to take that sacrifice upon ourselves, and not lay it on others if we can avoid doing so. By going early to bed, George will sacrifice mainly his own pleasure; but sleepiness and dulness or heaviness in the morning causes trouble both to mother and teachers.

"I imagine, however, that he has never looked at the matter in this light. I hope he will do so now, and conform his conduct to the true social order. The tendency to argue is a different point. Mrs. Plimsoll is right, it exists strongly in him; and in this case it appears to have led practically to an act of disobedience, for which there can be no justification. In my capacity of teacher "—this was an explanatory phrase directed to the strangers present,—" I observe character closely, and wilful disobedience is, I venture to say, no trait of George's. I am sure that the button, which certainly ought to have been sewed on and was not, does not indicate inward revolt against his mother's command, but ——." Here George started to his feet in a visible tremble of eagerness to speak. The chairman instantly raised a warning finger, and he subsided, and slowly re-seated himself—" rather I should say some mistaken mental impression, a sophistical one, doubtless, that proved consonant with the inclination of the moment, though counter to duty. I beg, therefore, for suspension of judgment on this misdemeanour till we hear him in his own defence.

"This leads me, however, to point out some defects of George's character, and perhaps they are dangers common to all intellects of dialectical tendency. Sophistry is one of these dangers, and another is forgetfulness of the practical in pursuit of the abstract."

The subject of criticism leaned forward at this point, and one could see that his kindling interest in the abstractions presented was deadening consciousness, not only in regard to his neglected button, but, also to the fact that his own personality was the object matter under Walter's dissection. " George's attention is strongly fixed on social institutions, their birth and parentage, or, to speak more correctly, their evolution; and although the bearing of these on the interests and well-being of working men was the starting and is still the central point of his inquiries, the whole phenomena are so complex, so brimful of opportunity for pleasurable exercise of

N—2

skill in penetrating mystery and unfolding labyrin-thine involvements that the student is sometimes caught in a snare, the phenomena he should grasp, grasps him, possesses him; he lavishes, nay exhausts his vital forces in a mere preparation for his true life-work! George, happily, on his own promptings, seeks counteracting influences; to be brought into contact with working men, to be taught a handicraft. If his life is perpetually touching the real at these two points, his tendency to stop short at the ideal will be suitably held in check. He must guard against injury to sight, but of this Dr. Basil intends to speak. Carpentry appears to me an occupation that would not try his eyes, and I trust our dear friend, his mother, will speedily see that her son's choice of profession is a confession of faith that evidences his gentle birth, that marks him, in short, the true gentle-man."

Dr. Basil was now about to speak, when Percy Cairns, in a shrill voice, said: "Papa, he can't be a gentleman always, he said so himself, I heard him, out there in the passage; his fingers will be dirty."

"My definition of gentleman, my boy," Walter replied gravely, "has to do with the heart and the mind, not the hands: but of course I should expect him to wash his hands after being engaged in dirty work."

"The strangers present to-night," said the doctor, "may not be aware that we carefully test the eyesight of the young at intervals, according to Priestley Smith's system, by letters adapted from the 'Opto-Typi' of Pro-fessor Snellen. Short-sight is caused chiefly by misuse of the eyes in youth.*

---

* Birmingham and Midland Institute "Lectures on Health," second series, No. 3. "Eyesight and how we Lose It," by Priestley Smith: price one penny.

" Now, for the last two months the test has enabled me to detect in George a slight tendency to the development of short-sight. It is my duty to check the evil. I am sorry to say he has not willingly aided my efforts in this matter. I forbade his use of the microscope, and of all small-printed books. Unfortunately, one or two of his favourite books are so printed, and relinquishing these was a source of inward irritation. I explained to him the necessity for my action as plainly as I could, and argued against his objections—that my command was too arbitrary, and that since his own eyes only were at stake he might do as he chose in the matter. Ultimately he submitted, but by giving way to a morbid vexation, his health suffered, and for some days his physical system was out of tone.

" I rejoice at his decision to take up manual labour as a special calling; the focus of his eyes is elongating, from book-work keeping them too much on the stretch, the handwork will prove a relaxation of tension.

" I need hardly say " (with a smile good humouredly directed to George) " that to thread a needle and sew on a button is not a dangerous process to his eyesight, although I guess, and even can sympathize with the bias of feeling that led to his thinking it might be dangerous."

Dr. Basil sat down, and the proceedings for the next five minutes fell, to the surprise of the strangers, into the hands of the critickins. Each child present had something to say for or against George's conduct, and each in his turn was respectfully listened to.

Harry complained, " He stews at his lessons, and once he said I would grow up a muff because I won't stew. I wish the doctor would tell me to give up books."

Jim mentioned that George, when let alone, was usually a good-natured fellow, but one day he got in a

terrible wax because Esther said, "George you are cross;
is your stomach out of order?" George said it was hateful to have it supposed that a fellow's stomach had
anything to do with his temper; and he wouldn't be friends
with Esther. He said she might as well have called him
unmanly at once. "I took Esther's part," said Jim, "for
she didn't mean anything of the sort, and he and I
almost quarrelled; but Ruth heard us, and asked if the
whole question couldn't be referred to the Conduct Club;
and we fixed that it could, and shook hands. So that
night we called a meeting, and had a splendid debate on
manliness. I never heard George speak so well, but he
gave in about Esther, and begged her pardon, and I think
myself that George *is* manly, for when he sees he is
wrong he always says so, and is never sneakish about
anything."

The evidence that followed was interesting as bearing
on George's domestic qualities, and his relations with his
young companions. It transpired that for the period of
a year he had been less zealous in sports than formerly,
and had betrayed what to some young minds seemed a
tiresome inclination to go off with a book at the play-hour.

The force of association, in unwittingly presenting poor
Harry to the shafts of criticism, appeared a second time in
Percy's artless announcement: "I like Harry best in the
play-ground, but George is ever so much nicer if you
want help in lessons. Harry never ——"

"Your likes and dislikes, my dear," his father interrupted, "are irrelevant. I told you the meaning of that
word this morning. We are not criticising Harry, and
what George is or does can be told without your likes and
dislikes."

Whilst Walter was saying this the door was opened, and

Margaret's head became visible. Vera rose, and quietly passed out; and Margaret, after a few whispered words in the passage, as quietly entered and took her place.

She was the next to address the meeting. " At George's request," she said, " I have to explain his wish to be taught the industry of a plumber. There are some of our children who regard this form of labour with special dislike, and taunted George with bad taste in choosing it. The subject gave rise to—not quarrelling exactly—but recrimination and anti-social feeling. In the end, a debate was decided upon, and all that could be said for or against plumbing freely discussed. I happened to be present, so was invited by the young people to take part, and as all my sympathies were with George in his defence of the trade, on the grounds of its supreme social importance, its as yet defective science, hence its scope for the exercise of intellectual skill as well as manual dexterity, he asked me to defend his position before you this evening. No opposition to his wish, as I understand, however, has been offered; therefore I need only relate some facts. During the last frost, when we were put to much inconvenience by the bursting of pipes, and the discovery that the imperfect water-pipe system adopted in the building of La Maison made it impossible to guard effectually against repetition of the disaster, some plumbers were at work here for several days, and George was permitted to watch them at work. It was then that he perceived the intricacies of household drainage and water supply, and learned to appreciate its difficulties, the need of reform, and the need of *con amore* workers in this humble sphere of reform. His resolve was taken, and he set himself to gain a conception of the amount of knowledge in the various departments—statics, dynamics or kinetics, hydrostatics, hydraulics, etc., he must acquire, before he could adequately grasp the problems in whose solution he was eager to assist. The vista of scientific study was appalling, and precisely at this crisis an embargo was laid on his free use of eyesight! To his ardent mind the trial was acute; and I give him credit, although Basil does not, for some little self-control in meeting it.

"His intellect is synthetic, rather than analytic, and the practical in him takes the form, at present, of planning his future, arranging, combining, uniting his ideas into a symmetrical whole. His synthesis, built on plumbing, was imposing! but behold the entire structure threatened by the doctor's caution! He must sacrifice something: to George it appeared the lesser evil, the more manly course, to sacrifice sight in pursuit of knowledge, of truth, of usefulness. Hence his obduracy, and when Basil convinced him he was wrong, a despondent mood laid hold of him, till I pointed out that renunciation of his whole enterprise is not called for.

"In our Commune we have no need to hurry our children into the business of life, or send them forth to the world ill equipped for its service. George's abilities are great; his development slow. Let him guard his sight, and train his hands in the use of tools of various kinds; meanwhile the books of small type he requires for his purpose are reprinting at my private expense, and I am glad of this opportunity of aiding, not the public only, but some authors whose poverty compelled them to do what publishers dictated as best for the market from the standpoint of profit alone.

"I have only one further remark: George is massive in sentiment as well as ideas. His affections are collective rather than individual. His sympathies flow out to the whole proletariat, his chivalry to the entire female sex, whilst he is apt to overlook the smaller matters of duty, of personal kindness to mother or sister, of domestic amenities, of human fellowship.

"I wish him to become more sensitive to immediate surroundings, and quick to respond to the mood of the moment in others,—less dreamy, in short, and I think this travelling with Mons. Martin and coming into direct contact with new personalities may enlarge his powers of adaptation, and help to individuate his trains of feeling."

Ruth made a few remarks *apropos* of his inattention to small matters, such as hanging his clothes in the proper place, brushing his shoes to perfection, etc., and Mr. Ray bore witness to some failings in respect of household proprieties; then George was called to his feet.

The boy rose slowly, put a hand in his pocket and balanced himself, first on one leg, then on the other. The impulse to self-defence had entirely left him. What he would have liked to do was argue on the point that a good plumber was a superior social unit to a good carpenter. He had not been satisfied with Margaret's speech. He had hoped the embargo would be removed from one or two of these small-typed books, on the ground of delay bringing injury to public interests when the business in hand was preparing a plumber champion for the people! He took his hand from his pocket and pushed back the hair from his forehead—there shot through his mind like an arrow, "But this is not a debate meeting, I must not argue," and looked down at his toes.

Suddenly he remembered to glance at a paper he held in his left hand, then looking straight at the Chairman, with a beautiful expression of simple childlike yet manly sincerity and candour, he said, "Oh, I forgot! When mother was speaking, I made up my mind to sew on the button. I ought to have done it before. I did not remember it this morning, and yesterday I thought mother would sew it on herself: she used to at Leeds, and it takes me so long to thread a needle. I suppose I am stupid to bungle so at that: it seems as though I couldn't learn. Oh! perhaps—don't you think it may be hereditary? Boys have never had to sew till now, and girls have always had to handle the needle. I did really think it might try my eyes; but mother isn't a bit anxious about my eyes, like she was when we had the measles. Short-sight is not a disease, she says, but Dr. Priestley Smith, in his pamphlet, calls it an unnatural condition from which people suffer; so I fancy it must be a disease, though 'suffer' can't mean much pain, for I have been asking short-sighted people, and they don't suffer pain. I don't want, though, to be short-sighted—I am glad Dr. Basil found it out; he's awfully clever. I didn't mean to vex him; I know it is his duty to keep us all well; and of course, prevention is better than cure. He told me "—and George's eyes sparkled, some fresh train of ideas of peculiar interest seemed to be set in motion—" that doctors will some day root out disease in the race by preventing it in individuals, and checking its inheritance. What a grand thing to do!" he exclaimed with enthusiasm.—" I'd like to be a doctor!" He had not this time forgotten the personal in the abstract.

"But no," he continued, with logical consistency, though indifference to grammar, " a doctor is a profession, not a people's trade. I must be a plumber, and one of themselves." He paused: the Chairman looked inquiringly at him, and he at his paper. Then again he began precisely as before.

"Oh, I forgot! About laziness: yes, I know I am lazy. I'm an awfully sleepy fellow in the mornings. I'll try that going to bed early. Oh! by the bye, if I got up early, perhaps I might read the book upon hydrostatics, though it is small print; the light is awfully good in the early morning, Basil said so himself."

Mr. Spiers interrupted with, "The Doctor can decide that question at another time," and George turned again to his paper.

"Mr. Cairns said I forget the practical in pursuit of the abstract, but Margaret said I am practical when I arrange my ideas: so I don't know what to think about that; but I know I often forget to do things that I ought, and I felt quite ashamed when Ruth told you all how untidy I am, I will try hard to improve, I want to behave better at home.

"If Blanche had been here, she would have complained I was unkind to her yesterday. I am awfully sorry: she teazed me when I was reading. How a fellow forgets to do right at the right time—" Another glance at the paper, then, "I don't know anything more to say. May I go with Monsieur Martin to Shipley? That won't try my eyes."

Down he sat suddenly, and the colour that came to his face showed that an excess of self-conscious feeling had overtaken him.

The Chairman, in a few pithy sentences, summed up the traits of character spoken of, the bad habits pointed out, the errors to be retrieved; then exhorted George to patient perseverance in self-improvement, and accepted, on the part of the meeting, his pledge to that effect. A report, he said, would be passed to the General Council, by whom he was authorised to state at once that George might accompany Monsieur Martin to Shipley.

The Criticism was over. It had occupied rather less than an hour. Mrs. Ward lay back on her sofa; the doctor drew up her wrappings and threw open a window. There was a bustle of movement and buzz of voices in the room for a few moments: the children went off to bed.

Then quietness reigned whilst Rose, at the piano, discoursed sweet music, and melody won the pulses of all to pleasurable vibration. At half-past nine the young people had dispersed, but a circle of elders remained. Whist was in process, and besides Mrs. Ward, Mrs. Oswald, and Mr. Ray, a new member sat at the table.

This new member is none other than our old friend, Mr. Scott. Some calamities of the kind that the rich are not exempt from any more than the poor had lifted him out of his old home of solitary grandeur, and placed him as permanent inmate in La Maison. His faithful housekeeper had "been called" as she herself had expressed it. A simple stone in the churchyard, a tender chord of memory within her old master's breast, these were the only records of a thirty years' service, of an obscure but patient and laborious life. Her master had not been similarly "called," yet a gentle reminder had reached him —a stroke from the hand of fate that to the wise man speaks of more to follow.

"The beginning of the end, I call this," he said to himself; "I will put my house in order." Had he meant to refer to his beautiful dwelling, where empty rooms stood garnished, but not swept, where dust had become conspicuous even to the eye of the unobservant, confiding, lonely bachelor, the resolve would have had its significance.

But it was to money he referred, and what to do with his money was a point of still greater difficulty. To provide for Vera and Vera's children, and bequeath the bulk of his fortune to public charities had been his intention when Vera married.

Mr. Scott had outlived his ideals. He was a disciple of Cobden and Bright; he had preached the Free Trade gospel, and plunged heart and soul into the Anti-Corn-Law agitation. Disillusion came quickly to him. Cheap food a panacea? Alas! alas! Were bread a penny a loaf, misery and squalor might sleep for the hour; they would not be slain. Production in every field increases, not least in that field that supplies the labour market; population advances by leaps and bounds; the market is glutted with hands; wages fall; women become slaves to the "law of eleven-pence halfpenny,"* and with mothers half starved, down goes the national pulse, the national health. Depression of trade brings depression of vitality; slowly but surely the race deteriorates, whilst the social problem remains as before.

In a period of trade depression and a mood of pessimism, Mr. Scott started for America. He visited the great cities there, and left them endorsing Mr. George's dictum: Progress and Poverty go hand in hand, and happiness is mocked in the new world as in the old.

He turned to Socialistic communities. The Shakers, Rappites, Perfectionists, Separatists, Icarians—he visited them all, but remained despondent still; their primitive life and simple principles scarce seemed to *touch* the broad questions of national poverty, of the manifold requirements of a civilised race.

Back again by his own fireside, Mr. Scott dropped into oblivion the great social problem, and cultivated contentment. Enterprise was with him a thing of the past.

* See Besant's " Children of Gibeon."

Even his business no longer required it. Firmly established and rooted in the country's industrial soil, it flourished and grew independently of its creator. In times of prosperity his profits rolled up; in times of adversity they fell, but never to a level that on *him* entailed a single personal sacrifice. Now, face to face with the end, as he thought, at no distant date, old doubts and difficulties beset him, and how to bestow the fortune with which Fate, not his labour or merits, had endowed him, was a perplexing question. He had been a constant spectator, and close observer of life in La Maison. From his standpoint of saddened experience, he bore with the idealism rampant there, treating it with gentle sarcasm, as generous folly—a feature of youth, whilst he kept a single eye to the happiness of his old friend's wife and child. So far as they were concerned, the experiment had been a success; and now he believed Vera's innocent heart would reject his fortune as she had rejected himself two years before. In his illness she had come to him, and the filial bond between them had immensely strengthened under the novel conditions of helpless dependence on his side, generous service on hers. So it came to pass that the Gordian knot of his dilemma was cut by her delicate fingers.

"What would you do with a great deal of money, my dear, if you had it?" he asked.

To his surprise her answer was prompt and decided.

"I would build a great wing to La Maison; and first, I would give you no rest, grandpapa, till you came to live with us in rooms we should make, oh! so beautiful, for your sake; then Ruth's sister, there would be room for her, and many more probationers. You know, we can only take six just now, and it is so sad, when people write and beg us to let them come and try our community life, we have to say No! What a terrible fate to be homeless, and if you ask for a home, to be refused!"

"And if you had more money still?"

"Ah! then, I would use it every penny in helping the people. I have gone lately many times with Joe, or with Margaret, to all the worst parts of Liverpool, and my heart has ached for the people."

Never had Mr. Scott seen so grave, so sweet an expression on Vera's face as when she said, "We long to teach them the Conduct of Life, poor things; they know nothing, how should they know? School board teaching is all about history, grammar, spelling, and perhaps a little cooking and sewing, but *very* little. No wonder their houses are airless, their children unhealthy, and often their manners rude. Once, long ago, I was made a district visitor, but just for a week. Oh! how I hated it. It seemed cruel for ladies in silks and finery to go to poor women in rags, and teaze them with tracts! A rough man was rude to me, I remember: what he said was, a poor man's house is his castle, and no one ought to come poking in there! His wife would be none the better of fine ladies coming about! But now it is different. Surely they will let us. We are not fine ladies; we are working women like themselves. See! my hands are rough—not very, to be sure; perhaps it would be better if we did not wear gloves—oh! I think they will let us, when they know how we feel; we hate the classes, not the people in the classes, you know, but the thing; we want no one to toil and struggle all their lives for daily bread, and then when their babies perhaps after all nearly starve "——

Vera choked a little, and became incoherent. "My own wee man is as fat, as fat——"

"But how do you mean to help these people, Vera? Are you going to build a Familistère?"

"No! no! you have not heard : it is since you were ill that our plans have been made.   Not a Familistère—they are not Socialists yet, but a Lecture Hall, something like that of the People's Palace, in London, a beautiful Lecture Hall we are going to build in their midst, and teach them, if we may, the Conduct of Life.   That means everything, you know—how to be good and happy husbands and wives, fathers and mothers, and children ; how to be clever housewives, and cooks and sick-nurses; how to dress well, and eat well, and sleep well; how to dance and sing and be cheerful, yet always gentle ; and best of all, how to be good citizens, full of public spirit, helping all of their order round and round to prepare for the change that is coming when competition and wage slavery will be over, and freedom for the people begin.   Have you heard Mr. Cairns and dear Frank speak to working men? They can do it so well; and Joe! my own Joe, he tried it last night.   We have hired a room till our own hall is built."

A doubtful look had come into Mr. Scott's eyes.   "If all you young women," said he, "go dancing after the poor in Liverpool, the dwelling at Peterloo will be neglected, and the old, not to speak of the babes ——"

"Oh dear! Oh dear! Just as if we could!" Vera merrily smiled up into his face, and as he smiled back, put her arms round his neck and kissed him with all the freedom and grace of girlish familiarity.   "You remind me of Joe in our courtship days.   He thought girls were only fit for embroidery and dressing in their best to receive company."   Laughter rippled from her lips.   "He knows better now.   He calls me as strong as a pony.

I love work ; as for embroidery and fal-lals! I loathe them."

"Poor ladies in the dark middle ages might be glad of their tapestry, but to-day, with art and science all about one, and ever so much real work waiting to be done, I call them an insult to our sex. Now look here, grandpapa. We have been almost two years in setting our house in order, but beautiful order it is—no rusty grates, as I see in your bedrooms up stairs! Poor Jane, we must not be hard on Jane. Her young man has run off to America, and forsaken her, so Sarah tells me; I daresay she cries her eyes out, and can't see the rust on your grates. You see they are yours, not hers ; and love is not in the case. Love, with her, poor thing, has folded his wings and fled. How I wish there were a Familistère, where she might be happy when I carry you off to La Maison—

"So you think we shall neglect you there. Ah! You don't know what love and co-operation can do. They are giants for work, and our love has grown so huge and strong, it is just like the giant Atlas bearing the globe on his shoulders and bending under the weight. The thought of the people, the suffering, toiling, patient people, weighs us down with grief. We stretch out our arms to them from our own beautiful home. We know how to live and love, now. We must show them how.

"We would work with them and for them, and teach them the Conduct of Life."

o

CHAPTER XIII.

SCIENTIFIC MELIORISM.

In one of the numerous provincial meetings which are indicative of the rapid progress of women in culture, thought, and independent spirit, a youthful advocate of freedom for her sex spoke thus: "When the poet tells us that woman's love to man's love is 'as water unto wine,' he speaks truth beyond his intention. Woman's love is wholesome, pure, and vivifying; man's, too often, the wine which is a mocker, and the strong drink which is raging."

Whether we accept this comment on the poet's words or not, I think it must be clear to us all that whilst the great world has been spinning " down the ringing grooves of change," the distinctive qualities of man and woman have broadened and deepened; hence they stand farther apart under civilisation than in barbarism. The reverse process has now, however, commenced. The currents of life are drifting them nearer. By and by, in a social environment in which the most powerful factor for the formation of character shall be these distinctive qualities of the sexes, man and woman will co-operate. Shoulder to shoulder they will fight the vicious tendencies of their time; hand in hand they will work and play, "and labour meet delight half way"; heart to heart they will pour

194

into each the gold of the other's nature, tried in the fire; and neither will be stinted of that rich inheritance—the broad humanity the ages have so patiently wrought out.

Frank Ray's nature had grown immensely in La Maison. His domestic instincts had budded and flowered, his emotional and moral forces strengthened, and the latter had become conscious. To measure the ratio of his advance with that of the women, whose lives were in daily contact with his, were an impossible task. Such comparisons are not only difficult, but at all times false. He gave forth as liberally as he received, and the healthy breezes from his manly, sensational nature lightly carried away the feminine tendencies to morbid sentimentality.

There was no breach between Margaret, Rose, and himself when they came together again after his absence abroad. The only change was one of knowledge, not of feeling; and the love that was nature's gift to all was reverently cherished by each.

A wealth of love is a simple necessity to the permanence and stability of an associated home; a selfish monopoly on the part of husband or wife is intolerable there; but observe, that is only one side of the picture. "Verily, a Community," says the *Altruist Journal* for June, 1886, "is a good place to be good, but at the same time it is equally as much of a bad place to be bad." Now, why is this? For the simple reason that with freedom of life and of love, and better social organisation, come also a multitude of wholesome checks—an innumerable host of delicate forces that will restrain the barbarous man, and keep pure and sweet the holy relations of life. No jealous pangs ever visited Rose; and I pause here to surmise, though I cannot know it as a fact, that were she cut off in her prime her most fervent desire would be that the vacant place in her husband's heart and life should be filled, in so far as nature will permit, by the friend beloved of both.

" There is a hiatus, Margaret, somewhere ;" said Frank, looking at her with the eye of an earnest philosopher, " all schemes for better social life, requiring an improved human nature, are only for realisation in the far future. What is wanted just now is such action as will effect an immediate improvement, however small, in the social sur- roundings; and so lead gradually, but surely, to better conditions for the whole mass of the people, which will have the result of beneficial re-action on the moral nature of the average man."

" Just so, dear Frank; I have felt very much what you say all along. Of the theories taught, some are not applicable to the preponderent human nature around us, but only to selected individuals here and there. Others are applicable to average human nature; but they can effect nothing until, through the slow advance of public opinion, the conditions requisite to put them in practice are brought about. To preach advanced Socialism in the back slums of Liverpool! is it not folly? The results must surely be, discontent in the heart, fierce revenge and hatred towards the dominant class, blind forces of revolu- tion aroused ——"

" You remind me," Frank interrupted, " of our debate last Sunday evening at Northampton. A shoemaker started to his feet at some allusion to society as a very complex machine, and with quite an aggressive tone, dared us to deny that society had been built from the foundation by his class—the working men, and the working men alone ! "

Frank had for some months been studying the working

man, although he could only devote the week-ends, so called, to this purpose. He had become familiar with the thoughts of the thinkers concerning work and life; he must now know the thoughts of the living workers themselves.

It was after a visit to Norwich, a town exceptionally strong in Socialism, that Frank joined his wife and friend in a joyous mood, and one slightly poetic, which was unusual with him. "I have found a new star in the sky, love," he said to Rose. "What are these lines you are fond of? They haunted me all the night :—'He who has found a new star in the sky,—Is not so fortunate as one who finds—A new, deep-hearted friend.' Yes, Margaret, a friend after *your* heart I have found: a philosopher! —not a mere anarchist, social democrat, communist, collectivist, socialist, or even Fabian; but one who is all these, and more. He has thought out the present condition of things, and has systematized a reform—I mean, a theory and practice immediately applicable! Our hiatus, Margaret, is filled by his—scientific meliorism.

"He is coming here soon. How you will delight in his clear insight; his backward and forward ken; his grasp of the present; his knowledge of social forces at work; of which of these forces ought to be strengthened, and which to be left to subside, so that quickly throughout society the general movement, guided, in the main, by human intelligence, leaving nothing out that is capable of control, shall go steadily in the direction of Socialism. Oh, yes! you will like him. You will see, eye to eye, you and he, —and I shall be jealous," he added, in the playful mood that betokens perfect confidence in your friend.

"His name, what is his name?" cried Margaret.

"It is Alfred Widnell, and here is his history as he told

it me in a tiny room in a back street at Norwich, where he took me to tea.

"'I have no home but this,' he said. 'I have lived in this one small room for six years past, uncomfortably, on about £1 a week, and devoted more than half my earnings to others. But, alas for progress! the need of funds is so urgent, and the rich give so little for the public good. What they do give, too, constantly goes in wrong directions —directions that tend to increase evil, to perpetuate this perplexingly unjust social state in which we all live, and so many starve. I cannot, for the life of me, see,' he continued, ' why a rich man could not live comfortably on half, or a quarter, of his income, and devote the remainder to the education of the people who are living in darkness and misery. My mind is continually passing between states of indignation and grief in the contemplation of the rich and the poor; the terrible contrast of what is with what might be.' I told him of you, Margaret, of what you have done, and what you are about to do. He had heard of our Commune, but he knew none of the details concerning your fortune, nor that we are prepared to spend all our surplus income in that work which he calls scientific meliorism. Then he asked if I had observed that lately two public-spirited aristocrats, already wealthy, had dropped into fortunes, which must have been unexpected. ' Will their consciences,' said he, ' permit, with the awful problem of poverty before them, that they simply increase the luxury of their, at present, most luxurious living, and forget all the claims of their suffering fellow-men?'"

"But, Frank," Rose asked earnestly, "does this Mr. Widnell live with a wife and children in one room?"

"No, I did not say he was married; he is a bachelor,

so must take care of himself, and doesn't do it over well, to judge by wan looks and a spare physique."

"Ah, Frank," Rose said, with a sudden impulse of sympathy, "we must get him to live with us. Mr. Spiers has had much better health, you know, since he came here. Don't you think it so sad that precious human life should ever lie neglected in desolate lodgings?"

"He calls himself"—Frank continued his relation—"a manual worker. He is really an artist employed by a picture dealer, and paid on the principle of piece-work. There are long intervals of no work, when he must remain close at hand, his employer losing nothing by the enforced idleness. 'I have lately finished,' he said, 'an oil painting, and received for my work £5 and a few shillings. That picture will sell for £20. Now, deducting all expenses—my wage, the frame, canvas, colours, allowing also a proportion for rent and taxes, the profit to my employer, on that picture alone, must be £10 at least, yet his work was simply taking the order and handing it over to me. The whole system of trade is odiously unjust. The larger incomes arise from superior chances and superior cunning, whilst superior skill, merit, industry, are nowhere in the running. But, for all that,' Mr. Widnell added, 'a better system will not succeed until scientific meliorism has paved the way.'"

It was a new life for the recluse, when, after the lapse of a few weeks, he joined the inmates of La Maison, and flung himself, heart and soul, into the practical work of scientific meliorism in a great centre of the world's industry on a scale likely to attract observation, and bring about imitation, hence, rapid advance on the path of progress.

"I knew of your scheme," he said to Miss José one evening, "but I feared the motives might be egoistic only.

I mean for the happiness of your own class. It is strange, but yet true, that the rich don't succeed in making themselves happy ; evolution has given us certain requirements that the isolated home can never supply. The consciousness of this is growing, and you had discovered the secret of the true remedy. You were bound to unite with congenial spirits, the gentle, the refined ; and if the experiment proved a success, so great would the happiness be you might well be excused if, enjoying it, you forgot the misery of others."

"Not for a moment," Miss José replied, "did we ever intend to live for ourselves alone. There was much to accomplish first, however : home comfort to secure, the financial position to understand and regulate, the emotional relations to establish. Then again, the most urgent need of the times is true education. Until our school was organised, and our children displaying the fruits of a socialised life and training, we had no right to assume the grave responsibilities of extended public action."

Mrs. Plimsoll here entered the room with a bustling activity in curious contrast to the gentle dignity of the two whom she addressed.

" By special request you are wanted at the Finance Committee Meeting going to begin," and she hurried them to the committee-room.

Economy, both in money and time, was a quality of Mrs. Plimsoll's character, which she made it her function to radiate forth in the circle of La Maison. Her small vanities had subsided in surroundings where her personal social position was never questioned. Her anxieties concerning her boys and their future had disappeared, and she was free to indulge all the generous activities of a kindly, though narrow nature. No one of the group was more eager than she to carry help to the poor; and her practical knowledge of the struggles of life, of the qualities essential in rising from poverty to comfort, formed an invaluable reserve fund, or capital, on which the more ignorant communists could draw. It was she who pointed out that £26 per annum was an ample sum to pay all penniless adult workers for clothing and pocket-money, and £13 for each child. The washing, travelling expenses, and occasional exceptional outlays are defrayed from the general funds. Thus there are ladies under the roof of La Maison, who work diligently for precisely the wage of an ordinary cook. Moreover, to these ladies the wage is an element of small interest, except in so far as from it they succeed in saving a few pounds to advance the great work of socialising mankind.

Emulation amongst the young, in the matter of dress, is entirely independent of fashion. It takes the direction of simplicity, neatness, becomingness, but above all, economy. Now, considering that the income of the Associated Home, as explained in Chapter VI, is already £2,200, and that there are no servants, no horses and carriages—the aged and invalids alone drive for pleasure and health,—seeing also that the living is simple, and the hospitality, although abundant, is equally simple, it is not surprising that a yearly surplus of £500 may be reckoned on for public work.

The comrades justly considered that they are not entitled to live at the expense of those outer workers who provide their food, clothing, coal, execute their washing, et cetera, without doing these workers some benefit in return; and this benefit, it was resolved, must be in accordance with their own highest ideals, made applicable, of course, to the actual condition of the workers.

Where organisation to some extent exists, they will aid its development. All lecturers on social topics are welcome guests at La Maison. Rest, refreshment, sympathetic converse, await them at all times at Peterloo; and many a dispirited teacher, alternating emotionally between pessimism and optimism, gets anchored there on scientific meliorism. Despair disappears on the one hand, fond illusion on the other; and duty, animated by melioristic belief, supported by brotherly sympathy and co-operation, becomes easy and glad.

The beautiful hall built at Margaret's expense, and endowed by Mr. Scott, is almost completed, and the temporary lecture-room, where our friends have made acquaintance with the inhabitants of the neighbourhood, is about to be closed.

I trust my language here is tolerably correct, for the chronicler of Margaret's good deeds must beware of archaic Political Economy! When old Mr. Ray, in the simplicity of his heart, said "Margaret has built this hall; let us call it after her,"—"I build the hall!" the girl exclaimed, "I! my dear sir; what nonsense:" and showing him her hands, with a merry smile, "they can't even handle a mason's trowel."

"Now, my child, be reasonable," persisted the old man, "your capital——"

"My capital—mine!" she again interrupted; "Mr. Fawcett says 'capital is the reward of abstinence.' What abstinence have I endured? These two years have I wanted for anything? Nay, have I not been rich in everything—yes, *everything* that I wanted? Capital," she added with a graver air, "is a result of labour——"

On the eve of their fresh departure, the deliberations were frequent and earnest. Mrs. Plimsoll held the distinct opinion that a conference with mothers was the very first step in scientific meliorism. Political and social lectures, science classes,—these might be all very well, though for her part she didn't think much of them: " but when real reform begins, it will begin with the mothers. That man of yours, Frank, at Northampton!—it was like the conceit of his sex, to think Society built up by the working-men : I say it is built by the mothers; and I would keep the men out of our hall until all the women have been there, and know how we feel with them, and think for them, and what we would have them to do. There are delicate matters for mothers alone. They must limit their families. They must learn what their duty is to their own health, the health of their children, and the health of the nation. We women will instruct them in self-respect, and show them how to support one another in cases where men are brutal and ought to be resisted."

The conference with mothers was decided on, and in addition to verbal teaching, the tract entitled "Plain words to Mothers," written by Mrs. Ward and Mrs. Plimsoll, was distributed in hundreds of thousands, and carried from that centre to the bounds of the earth.

When the poor mothers were no longer isolated, but united in social feeling, another step was taken, viz., the formation of Conduct Clubs ; and the subtle forces of public opinion, gentle remonstrance, and friendly support, were brought to bear upon the unruly throughout the district.

A hint is given by a husband or a wife that the life companion is frequenting the public-house too frequently. A stronger member of his or her Conduct Club goes to the weaker member's rescue, and wherever the wish to reform exists, straying feet are quickly restored to the path of sobriety without interference of officialism—a coercive police.

It was not till the spring of 1894 that the Hall, whose interior had been embellished by the artistic work of Arthur Widnell and others of the comrades, and the exterior by a tower containing musical bells, was declared open to the general public for the teaching of scientific meliorism—a subject which embraces the rendering of humanity gentle and refined; the enlarging and improving of domestic life; the rationalizing of education and training; the organising of industry, and the whole field of labour; and the socialising of general society.

"Our lines of practical action," so say the Liverpool scientific meliorists, following Mr. Patrick Geddes' classification, are in terms of the successive sciences :—

(1.) Physical, concerned with wealth, and organisation of labour ;

(2.) Biological, concerned with health, and surroundings ;

(3.) Psychological, concerned with education ;

(4.) Social, and Political ;

(5.) Moral.

Hence the bells that were Rose's delight and Margaret's joy did not for the first time—"ring out to the wild night," not yet "across the snow."

The evening was soft in the pleasant month of May, and everywhere summer gave promise of approach, when a gay peal rang forth its invitation to the people to come.

In one of those quick transitions of mood to which youth is ever subject, Margaret dropped on her knees by

Miss José's side, and turning to her comrades, quoted in grave, sweet tones:

" Ring out the old, ring in the new.

*   *   *   *   *

Ring out the false, ring in the true,
Ring out the grief that saps the mind.

*   *   *   *   *

Ring in redress to all mankind.

" Ring out a slowly dying cause,
    And ancient forms of party strife;
    Ring in the nobler modes of life,
With sweeter manners, purer laws.

" Ring out false pride in place and blood,
    The civic slander and the spite ;
    Ring in the love of truth and right,—
Ring in the common love of good.

" Ring out old shapes of foul disease ;
    Ring out the narrowing lust of gold ;
    Ring out the thousand wars of old.

*   *   *   *   *

" Ring in the valiant man and free,
    The larger heart, the kindlier hand ;
    Ring out the darkness of the land,
Ring in the ' joy ' that is to be."

LONDON :

PRINTED BY CHAS. STRAKER & SONS, LIMITED,

5 TO 9, BISHOPSGATE AVENUE, CAMOMILE STREET, E.C.

CPSIA information can be obtained at www.ICGtesting.com
Printed in the USA
LVOW05s1739130814

398969LV00008B/356/P

9 781241 406417